FAITH CLINIC

VOLUME XXX
- MENTAL/EMOTIONAL EDITION -
"Check Your Pulse, The Body of Christ Is Flatlining"

DR. PATRICIA S. TANNER

©Copyright 2026

IBG Publications, Inc.

Published by I.B.G. Publications, Inc., a Power to Wealth Company

Web address: www.ibgpublications.com

admin@ibgpublications.com / 904-419-9810

IBG Publications, Inc., Jacksonville, FL

ISBN: 978-1-971850-18-4

Tanner, Patricia S.

Faith Clinic, Volume XXX- Mental/Emotional Edition-
"Check Your Pulse, The Body of Christ Is Flatlining"

Printed in the United States of America.

DEDICATION

To the weary souls exhausted by maintaining the perfect story, and to every heart that has used a lie as a shield against the pain of honesty.

This book is dedicated to those who are ready to dismantle the false personas, to stop hiding chaos behind curated perfection, and to finally admit that the devil didn't *make* them do it, fear did.

To the believers who choose radical, painful truth over comfortable deception, finding the freedom that only the Spirit of Truth can provide.

And most of all, to **Jesus Christ**, the Word made Flesh, whose truth is our authority, and whose blood cleanses the shame that silence breeds.

Your Faith Practitioner and friend,

DR. PATRICIA S. TANNER
The Faith Doctor

ACKNOWLEDGMENTS

To my Great Physician, Dr. Jesus, thank You for writing every chapter before I lived it. For refusing to let me self-diagnose my pain or medicate my pride. For calling me back when I mistook control for courage, and independence for identity.

To the Holy Spirit, my Counselor and Care Partner, thank You for every whisper, every nudge, every quiet correction that shaped these pages into healing. You are the steady voice in my chaos.

To my family, thank you for loving me through every rewrite, every late night, and every emotional ICU moment of this book's creation. You are my first ministry and my forever reminder that healing is a group project.

To every reader who's ever walked through their own faith rehab, thank you for showing up to your own recovery. You are proof that God still specializes in stubborn patients.

And finally, to every woman and man who's ever looked in the mirror and said, "I shouldn't still be here"… You're right, but grace decided otherwise.

TABLE OF CONTENTS

Welcome To The Clinic

"Because pretending you're fine won't stop the flatline."
Take a seat. Breathe. You made it to the Faith Clinic, where spiritual symptoms finally get the attention your Sunday smile has been hiding. This isn't your typical wellness retreat, and I'm not handing out peppermint-scented scriptures to make you feel better. You've checked in for a **Spiritual Body Exam**, which means we'll be poking, pressing, and possibly performing open-heart surgery on your faith. Don't worry, the Great Physician is in, and His bedside manner is flawless.

Here is the reality: The **Body of Christ** is brilliant in design but struggling in function. It's not that the heart has stopped beating, it's that the pulse has grown faint. The Church is moving, but not alive. Talking, but not breathing. Reacting, but not responding. Somewhere between revival conferences and self-help sermons, we've forgotten how to check our spiritual vitals.

The truth? You might have **heart disease** from loving ministry more than God. Maybe your **lungs** are shallow from years of singing louder instead of surrendering deeper. Perhaps your **nerves** are fried, too many stress signals, not enough peace. Or your **bones** ache from carrying burdens God never prescribed. This isn't punishment. It is a **diagnosis**. And every diagnosis is a doorway to deliverance, if you'll stop arguing with the Doctor long enough to let Him operate.

Before we start, let's be honest about a few things:
- You've ignored your symptoms. (Denial doesn't count as discernment.)
- You've self-diagnosed with "just tired," when you're spiritually **malnourished**.
- You've called emotional numbness "peace," but that's not calm, that's cardiac arrest.

- You've mistaken church attendance for checkups and service for healing.

You've been functioning on spiritual adrenaline, caffeine faith, not covenant faith. That is why your worship feels winded and your prayer life keeps flatlining. The Holy Spirit has been paging you for follow-up appointments you keep rescheduling in the name of "busy." Consider this your last reminder: **it's time for your exam.**

Here at the Faith Clinic, we don't hand out sugar-coated verses or soft affirmations. We do blood work on your belief system. We check the heartbeat of your humility, the reflexes of your obedience, the strength of your backbone, and the circulation of your love. If something's infected, expect exposure. If something's broken, expect it to be set, and yes, that might hurt. We practice **spiritual medicine**, not religious sedation. Every system in your natural body reflects a system in the **Body of Christ**.

Your **heart**? That's love and compassion. Your **lungs**? That's worship and breath. Your **bones**? That's doctrine and stability. Your **nerves**? That's sensitivity to the Spirit. Your **digestive system**? That's how you process and apply truth. And your **immune system**? That's discernment, protecting you from deception. If one organ malfunctions, the whole body feels it. The same goes for the Church. When the eyes (discerners) close, the hands (servants) stumble. When the mouth (preachers) speak without the Head's instruction, confusion spreads like infection.

The problem isn't that the Body's dead, it's that it's **disconnected**. And disconnection always leads to dysfunction. So yes, this exam is going to be uncomfortable. We'll test your **spiritual reflexes**, how you react when God says "wait." We'll measure your **blood pressure**, how quickly offense raises it. We'll examine your **lungs**, whether you breathe grace or release gossip. And we'll check your **heart rhythm**, is it beating for approval or intimacy? If you're already defensive, congratulations, the medicine is working. Healing rarely starts with "amen." It usually begins with "ouch." But stay with me. You're not here by accident. God scheduled this appointment before your breakdown, your burnout, and your spiritual silence. He's not here to condemn; He's here to **revive** what's gone faint. You just must stay at the table long enough for the surgery to finish.

In this Faith Clinic, we operate under one principle: "He sent out His word and healed them; He rescued them from the grave." Psalm 107:20 (NIV) That's the Doctor's order. The Word is the scalpel. Conviction is anesthesia. And transformation is the healing. So, let's begin the exam. Your pulse talks more about your faith than your post. Your spiritual bloodwork will reveal more than your Sunday outfit. And your vitals, those daily patterns of thought, emotion, and obedience, will show whether you're alive or just busy.

Grab your clipboard. Fill out the intake form honestly this time. No more "I'm fine." No more "It's just stress." You're in the clinic now, and **He's not checking symptoms, He's after the source.**

Faith Clinic Intake Form

"Because you can't heal what you keep hiding."
Department: Spiritual Diagnostics |
Edition: Mental/Emotional – Spiritual Body Exam
Attending Physician: Dr. Jesus, Chief Physician of Hearts
Nurse on Duty: The Holy Spirit (warning: He's very direct)

Patient Information
Full Name: ___________________________________
(*Or the name you hide behind at church*)
Date of Salvation (if applicable): _______________
(*Approximate is fine, we'll pull your records from Heaven's databa*)

Spiritual Status (check all that apply):
☐ Revived but tired
☐ Saved but salty
☐ Forgiven but frustrated
☐ Anointed but anxious
☐ Called but confused
☐ Walking by faith… limping a little
☐ Prefer not to say (aka "still under construction")

Emergency Contact: ___________________________
(*Who do you call when conviction hits, your prayer partner or your comfort sin?*)

Primary Church or Fellowship: _________________
(*We ask because community health affects your recovery speed.*)

Presenting Symptoms
(*Please be honest, lying on this form delays your healing.*)
☐ Emotional fatigue (also known as spiritual anemia)
☐ Difficulty breathing during worship (possible praise blockage)

☐ Heart palpitations when confronted with truth
☐ Stiff neck from resisting correction
☐ Vision problems, unable to see God's perspective
☐ Hearing loss, selective obedience disorder
☐ Digestive issues, sermon intake with no application
☐ Numbness, desensitized to the Holy Spirit
☐ Overreaction, spiritual nervous system malfunction
☐ Poor circulation, no flow of grace to others
☐ Memory loss, forgot who you are in Christ
☐ Joint pain, disconnected from the Body
If *"all of the above"*, please proceed directly to **intensive care (a.k.a. repentance).**

Spiritual Medical History Past Diagnoses:

☐ Pride (chronic)
☐ Comparison syndrome
☐ Perfectionism disorder
☐ Fear of failure
☐ Approval addiction
☐ Church hurt infection
☐ Control issues (severe)
☐ Unforgiveness buildup
☐ Doubt deficiency
☐ Unchecked idolatry

Previous Surgeries:

☐ Circumcision of the heart (Romans 2:29)
☐ Brokenness procedure (Psalm 34:18)
☐ Pruning operation (John 15:2)
☐ Deliverance detox
☐ Ego removal (pending follow-up)

Current Medications (spiritual disciplines):
☐ Daily Scripture dose (frequency?) _______________
☐ Prayer regimen (consistent / inconsistent / emergency only)
☐ Worship therapy sessions (corporate / private / rare)
☐ Fellowship vitamins (active / allergic to accountability)

Known Allergies:
☐ Correction
☐ Waiting seasons
☐ Silence from God
☐ Saying "I was wrong"
☐ Letting go of control

Diagnostic Questions
1. When was the last time you checked your **spiritual pulse**, not your platform stats?
2. How often do you confuse **busyness with fruitfulness**?
3. Are you breathing grace or inhaling gossip?
4. Does conviction make you defensive or desperate for change?
5. Which system of your spiritual body feels weak, your heart (love), your mind (peace), your bones (conviction), or your breath (prayer)?
6. Are you currently **in community**, or are you a detached organ hoping to survive alone?
7. What do you run to when you feel unwell, Jesus or distractions?
8. Have you been skipping appointments with the Great Physician?

Faith Vital Signs

Vital	Normal Range	Your Reading	Doctor's Note

Love Flow	Unconditional	__________	"Needs transfusion" / "Stable"
Peace Pressure	Steady & calm	__________	"Elevated by anxiety"
Prayer Rate	Daily rhythm	__________	"Irregular; needs monitoring"
Word Intake	Balanced diet	__________	"Malnourished" / "Overfed, under-applied"
Humility Levels	Low self, high Christ	__________	"Critically low"
Gratitude Levels	Overflowing	__________	"Inconsistent"

Insurance Coverage Primary Coverage:

☐ Grace Unlimited (Romans 5:20)

☐ Works-Based Plan (expired at Calvary)

☐ Self-Sufficiency PPO (not accepted here)

Co-pay: Obedience.

(*Paid daily through surrender. No refunds.*)

Informed Consent

By signing below, you acknowledge that:

- Healing may cause discomfort.
- Truth may sting before it saves.
- The Holy Spirit reserves the right to reorder your life without prior notice.
- God's Word is the only approved medication.
- You may experience side effects such as peace, conviction, clarity, and uncontrollable worship.

Patient Signature: ________________________________

Date: ________________________________

(*Welcome to the process. You're in good hands, literally.*)

Faith Clinic Vitals Chart

"Because your spirit's numbers say more than your Sunday words."

Patient: ____

Date/Time: ___________________________

Exam Type: Full-Body Spiritual Assessment

Attending Physician: Dr. Jesus, M.D. ("Miracle Distributor")

Chart Nurse: Holy Spirit R.N. (Registered Nudger)

Status: ☐ Stable   ☐ Under Observation   ☐ Critical   ☐ Flatlining (Revival Required)

1. Heart Rate = Love Level

Normal Range: Steady affection toward God + people.

Reading: _________ BPM ("Beats Per Mercy").

Interpretation:

- Below 60 = Cold Love Syndrome (Matt 24:12)
- Over 120 = Performance Palpitations (Doing more than being)

  Prescription: Repent of resentment; let grace recirculate (Eph 3:17–19).

2. Respiratory Rate = Prayer & Worship Breath

Normal Range: 12–20 breaths of gratitude per minute.

Reading: _________

Interpretation:

- Shallow = Living on lyrics without presence.
- Rapid = Anxious hyperventilation from control issues.

  Prescription: Inhale Scripture, exhale surrender (Ps 150:6).

3. Neurological Response = Obedience Reflex

Normal Range: Immediate response to the Head (Christ).
Test: When convicted, do you flinch or follow?
Result: ☐ Delayed   ☐ Numb   ☐ Overreactive   ☐ Responsive
Prescription: Reconnect to the Head (Col 1:18); nerve repair via daily listening.

4. Skeletal Integrity = Doctrine & Conviction

Normal Range: Solid belief structure with flexibility for grace.
Findings: __________
Possible Conditions : Spineless Faith or Rigid Religion.
Prescription: Calcium of Consistency (Heb 10:23); stretch in truth and love.

5. Digestive Function = Word Application

Normal Range: Digest and absorb Scripture daily.
Symptoms: ☐ Sermon bloating   ☐ Word vomit   ☐ Malnutrition
Prescription: Chew slowly (Josh 1:8), swallow obedience, avoid empty calories of comparison.

6. Immune Defense = Discernment

Normal Range: Immediate rejection of false teaching & toxic thoughts. **Reading:** __________
If low: You may be suffering from Doctrinal Deficiency Disorder.
Prescription: Vitamin Word (2 Tim 3:16–17) + Immunity Boost of Community (Eph 4:14–16).

7. Hormonal Balance = Emotional Regulation

Normal Range: Peace governs feelings, not the other way around.
Reading: ☐   Stable   ☐   Irritable   ☐   Spiritually   hangry
Prescription: Fruit of the Spirit therapy (Gal 5:22–23); limit intake of drama.

8. Hydration Status = Presence of the Holy Spirit

Normal Range: Overflowing rivers (John 7:38).

Current Level: ☐ Dehydrated ☐ Half Full ☐ Overflowing
Prescription: Drink deeply from Living Water daily.

Doctor's Note "Your vitals show intermittent faith flow and mild obedience fatigue. Recommend immediate heart realignment, hydration through worship, and a follow-up appointment at the altar."

Discharge Instructions

1. Take the Word three times daily, before opinions, after offense, and at bedtime.

2. Replace anxiety with gratitude reps.

3. Keep your Body connected; isolation causes organ failure.

4. Schedule regular check-ins with the Great Physician.

5. Expect full recovery, prognosis: *Healed and Whole.*

Reflections

____

____

____

____

____

____

INTRODUCTION

The Body Is Beautiful, Until It Stops Functioning

Have you ever noticed that you don't really think about your heart until it skips a beat? You don't appreciate your lungs until your breath gets shallow. You don't consider your spine until it hurts to stand up. The human body, that incredible, intricate system of systems, can function on autopilot for years… until something stops working. Then, suddenly, everything else in the body adjusts, compensates, or collapses in response. That's exactly what's happening to the Body of Christ.

The Church, this divine organism God designed to breathe, move, and multiply, has been experiencing system failure. We still look alive: lights flashing, choirs singing, hands lifted. But underneath showmanship, there are weak pulses, shallow breaths, and chronic symptoms that point to something deeper, a spiritual body that's been ignoring its own warning signs. We've mistaken performance for health. We've replaced breath with noise. We've traded nourishment for inspiration. And in doing so, we've turned a living, breathing Body into a busy, limping one.

If you've ever wondered why the Church seems exhausted, divided, or spiritually dehydrated, it's because, just like a physical body, when one system is sick, the whole body suffers. God created both the human body and the spiritual Body of Christ with astonishing precision. Every part affects every other part. The body's health depends on harmony. And just like our organs, the Church's members were never designed to function alone.

Let's take a closer look at the parallels, not to glorify anatomy, but to reveal how heaven's blueprint for the human body mirrors the spiritual blueprint for the Church.

THE CIRCULATORY SYSTEM, THE FLOW OF LOVE AND LIFE

In your physical body, the circulatory system pumps blood into every cell, delivering oxygen and removing waste. When the heart stops beating, everything else shuts down. In the spiritual Body of Christ, love is that lifeblood. It keeps grace circulating, relationships oxygenated, and forgiveness flowing freely. But when love hardens, arteries clog. When bitterness builds, flow slows. Gossip, offense, and pride become spiritual cholesterol, and before long, the Church finds itself in cardiac arrest, active, but not alive.

A healthy circulatory system doesn't pick favorites. It sends life everywhere, even to the most wounded parts. The same is true in the Kingdom: you can't say you love God while withholding forgiveness from His people. *"The entire law is fulfilled in keeping this one command: 'Love your neighbor as yourself.'" (Galatians 5:14)*

When the Body stops circulating love, it doesn't need new programs, it needs **spiritual CPR**: Confession, Prayer, and Repentance.

THE RESPIRATORY SYSTEM, WORSHIP AS BREATH

Your lungs don't just keep you alive; they keep you balanced. Every inhale brings in what's needed; every exhale releases what's toxic.

The Holy Spirit functions much the same in the Church. He is the breath of God, filling us with truth and cleansing us through worship. But some believers are on spiritual life support, gasping for oxygen while surrounded by smoke from burnout. We sing about revival while holding our breath during conviction. We've forgotten that worship isn't the song; it is oxygen.

When worship is real, it's rhythmic: inhale presence, exhale praise. It's less about volume and more about flow. *"Let everything that has breath praise the Lord." (Psalm 150:6)* Because when the Church stops breathing in God's Spirit, it starts suffocating on its own ego.

THE NERVOUS SYSTEM, RESPONDING TO THE HEAD

The nervous system carries messages from the brain to every part of the body. One thought, one signal, and every nerve responds. When that connection breaks, the body becomes paralyzed or numb.

In the Body of Christ, Jesus is the Head. Every thought originates from Him, and every believer should respond in sync. But somewhere along the way, we stopped listening to the signals. We became reactionary instead of responsive, emotional instead of obedient. When one part of the Church moves without the Head's command, we call it independence. But heaven calls it spiritual nerve damage, a disconnect that numbs our discernment and delays our obedience. *"He is the head of the body, the church." (Colossians 1:18)*

A healthy nervous system doesn't argue with the brain, it carries the message immediately. The Body of Christ must relearn that reflex: to respond quickly when the Spirit speaks, not days later when it's convenient.

THE SKELETAL SYSTEM, STRUCTURE, STRENGTH AND STABILITY

Without bones, your body collapses. Without spiritual structure, biblical foundation, accountability, and truth, the Church does too. The skeletal system gives posture, alignment, and balance. Likewise, doctrine and conviction hold up the spiritual Body. But in today's culture, we've traded backbones for wishbones, wishing for blessing without structure, wanting miracles without maturity.

When the Church avoids the Word because it's "too strict," the bones grow brittle. When we replace holiness with hype, the spine of truth fractures. *"Do not be conformed to this world, but be transformed by the renewing of your mind." (Romans 12:2).* A sturdy Church isn't built on emotional worship but on unshakable truth. Because no matter how pretty the skin (the presentation), a spineless body can't stand under pressure.

THE DIGESTIVE SYSTEM, FEEDING AND APPLYING THE WORD

Your digestive system doesn't just take in food, it breaks it down, processes it, and turns it into energy. If it doesn't digest properly, you can eat all day and still be weak.

Spiritually, the same is true. The Church is overfed but undernourished. We binge on sermons, snack on devotionals, and scroll through spiritual quotes but rarely digest the Word deeply enough to fuel change*"Man shall not live on bread alone, but on every word that comes from the mouth of God." (Matthew 4:4)*

True spiritual digestion looks like meditation, reflection, and application, not just inspiration. The goal isn't to hear more, but to **become more.** Until we digest truth, it can't build spiritual muscle.

THE IMMUNE SYSTEM, DISCERNMENT AND DEFENSE

Your immune system identifies threats and fights them off. Spiritually, that is the role of discernment in the Body of Christ. But many believers have suppressed immune systems, easily infected by false teaching, emotional manipulation, and spiritual trends.

Discernment doesn't make you judgmental; it makes you *healthy*. Without it, the Body starts attacking itself, believers criticizing believers, churches competing with churches, and infections spreading unchecked. *"Test the spirits to see whether they are from God." (1 John 4:1)*. Discernment is Heaven's antibody. It doesn't just detect lies; it protects love.

THE ENDOCRINE SYSTEM, EMOTIONAL REGULATION IN THE SPIRIT

Your endocrine system manages hormones, maintaining internal balance. Spiritually, this is where the **Fruit of the Spirit** comes in, love, joy, peace, patience, kindness, goodness, faithfulness, gentleness, and self-control. But many saints suffer from hormonal imbalance, high highs of revival followed by low lows of disillusionment. Emotional instability has replaced spiritual maturity. The same people who shout "Hallelujah!" on Sunday are ghosting God on Wednesday. A balanced believer doesn't live on adrenaline; they live on alignment. The Holy Spirit stabilizes the soul's mood swings by reminding us that peace isn't a feeling, it is a fruit.

WHEN ONE SYSTEM FAILS, THE WHOLE BODY FEELS IT

If your physical heart stops, your lungs panic. If your lungs collapse, your brain suffers. The same is true in the Body of Christ. When one member is offended, the rest should feel the pain. When one church is thriving, the others should feel the joy. But we've grown so disconnected that compassion barely circulates anymore.

The Church isn't dying, it's **dehydrated**. It doesn't need more adrenaline; it needs alignment. It doesn't need bigger platforms; it needs better posture. Because when the Body of Christ operates like the human body, each system supporting the next, the world sees health, not hype. *"From him the whole body, joined and held together by every supporting ligament, grows and builds itself up in love."* *(Ephesians 4:16)*. The Master Physician never designed His Body to limp into glory. He designed it to move, breathe, respond, and radiate health. So, before we start shouting for revival, we need to check our vitals. Because the issue isn't that the Body has stopped existing, it's that it's forgotten how to function.

Welcome to your exam. The chart's waiting. The Doctor is in. And yes, the truth may sting a little, but that's how healing starts.

Chapter 1:

Code Blue, When The Heart Stops Loving

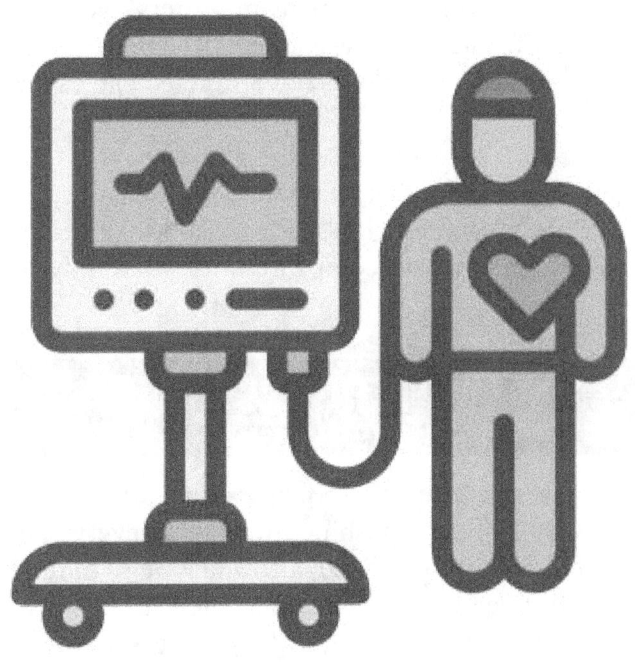

SYMPTOM: Spiritual Cardiac Arrest

 The monitors are beeping, the alarms are screaming, and everyone's scrambling for paddles. The patient? The Body of Christ. Diagnosis? Love depletion. You can always tell when the heart of the Church is failing, forgiven, failing out, patience drops, and compassion flatlines. The pulse of kindness grows faint while offense pumps faster than grace. People start serving God out of muscle memory instead of mercy, clapping on Sunday but clenching their fists by Tuesday. Just like the human body cannot live without constant circulation, the Church cannot survive without love. When the heart hardens, everything downstream suffers. Ministries lose oxygen. Families suffocate under resentment. Relationships turn blue around the edges because the blood flow of grace can't reach them anymore.

The Church doesn't need another adrenaline shot of hype; it needs a heart transplant. The rhythm of God's love must be restored, or every other system will fail trying to compensate for what only the heart can do.

TEACHING: The Circulatory System Of The Kingdom

In the human body, the heart never takes a day off. It beats about 100,000 times every 24 hours, pushing lifeblood to every cell. That's how the Body of Christ was designed, a constant pulse of divine love sending mercy, forgiveness, and encouragement to every believer. But when spiritual arteries clog with **unforgiveness, pride, or fear**, the flow slows down. The Church develops emotional cholesterol: self-centeredness thickens the blood, comparison calcifies the vessels, and before long, unity goes into cardiac arrest. The worship still sounds good, but the pulse is weak.

Jesus warned of this in Matthew 24:12: *"Because of the increase of wickedness, the love of most will grow cold."* Cold love equals poor circulation. Warmth leaves the extremities first, meaning we lose compassion for those farthest from our comfort zone. The "hands" (service) stop reaching; the "feet" (missions) stop moving; the "mouth" (witness) goes silent.

When a heart attack hits the human body, the rest of the systems collapse in seconds. Likewise, when love collapses in the Body of Christ, every ministry downstream suffers, outreach loses joy, preaching loses gentleness, and believers lose empathy. Paul wrote, *"If I have not love, I am nothing."* (1 Corinthians 13:2) Nothing. Not almost. Not partially. Completely non-functional. So, what does spiritual CPR look like?

C – *Confession*: Acknowledge where your heart has hardened.
P – *Prayer*: Invite God to restart your compassion.
R – *Repentance*: Turn from emotional apathy and let the blood of Christ flow freely again. You can't fake pulse. You can preach, sing, or post about revival, but if love isn't circulating, heaven still calls it a flatline.

Faith Prescription: Heaven'S Cardiac Care Plan

1. **Daily Heart Check:** Ask, "Who have I stopped loving?" Not who annoys you least, but who you've quietly placed on life support in your mind. Write their name down and pray life over them.

2. **Lower Spiritual Cholesterol:** Cut out gossip, comparison, and complaint. They thicken the blood of community. Replace them with gratitude and intercession.

3. **Increase Oxygen Flow:** Spend time in worship that focuses on God's nature, not your needs. Breath in His presence, exhale bitterness.

4. **Take the Word as Blood Thinner:** Read 1 Corinthians 13 every week until it stops sounding poetic and starts sounding practical.

5. **Exercise Love Muscles:** Serve someone who can't repay you. Nothing unclogs arteries faster than selfless acts.

Follow this regimen daily. Side effects may include peace, humility, and uncontrollable compassion.

Holy Spirit Consult

Doctor's Note: I've examined your charts, and the rhythm is irregular. You've been pumping performance instead of presence. You pray out of duty but not delight. You love those who love you but avoid those who need you. I can restart the heart, but you must stay still long enough for Me to shock it." The Holy Spirit specializes in defibrillation. He doesn't replace your heart; He revives it. But revival only works on what's surrendered. Lay down on the table and let Him restore the beat you lost when busyness replaced intimacy.

Guided Prayer

"Great Physician, I confess I've let my love grow cold. I've allowed disappointment and pride to block the flow of grace through me. Create in me a clean heart and renew the right spirit within me. Teach me to love beyond comfort, to forgive before being asked, and to serve without seeking credit. Shock my heart back into rhythm with Yours. Let Your love circulate through every chamber of my soul until compassion becomes my reflex again. In Jesus 'name, amen."

Reflection Page

1. Where have you felt "numb" toward people God keeps bringing into your path?

____

____

____

2. What situations reveal your love deficit the fastest, confrontation, correction, or inconvenience?

____

____

____

3. If love is the bloodstream of the Body of Christ, what's currently clogging your arteries?

____

____

____

4. How can you intentionally "circulate grace" this week, especially to someone you'd rather avoid?

____

____

____

5. Record a moment when you felt God's love pumping freely through you. What restored that rhythm?

Diagnostic Reminder: Healing begins the moment you admit you've lost your pulse. Stay for observation, the next system depends on a beating heart.

Reflections

Chapter 2:

Out Of Breath, When Worship Becomes Wheezing

SYMPTOM: Shallow Breathing In The Spirit

Somewhere between the pressure to perform and the exhaustion of pretending, the Church forgot how to breathe. The symptoms are everywhere: panic when silence hits, gasping for spiritual air between worship sets, and prayer that sounds more like panting than communion. The Body of Christ is wheezing, not from weakness, but from **spiritual overexertion without oxygen intake**.

In the natural body, your respiratory system takes in oxygen and releases carbon dioxide, the exchange that keeps you alive. Spiritually, worship is that exchange. When you inhale God's presence and exhale surrender, your spirit stays oxygenated. But many believers are holding their breath, trying to appear strong while suffocating in stress, pride, or performance. The result? Hypoxia of the soul. The symptoms? Anxiety masquerading as anointing. Busyness replacing breath. Singing louder to compensate for the silence in your spirit. We can't keep preaching about fresh fire if we refuse to breathe in fresh air. Revival can't flow through a Body that's spiritually short of breath.

TEACHING: The Respiratory System Of Worship

In **Genesis 2:7**, *"the LORD God formed man from the dust of the ground and breathed into his nostrils the breath of life."* The very first function of humanity wasn't speech or movement, it was breathing. God's breath animated Adam; His Spirit activated life. The Church was meant to live the same way, inhaling the presence of God, exhaling praise and obedience. The respiratory system's job is rhythmic: inhale, exhale. Take in what gives life; release what kills it. Spiritually, that means taking in truth and letting go of sin, pride, and anxiety.

But most believers are either hyperventilating or suffocating.

- **Hyperventilation** happens when we rush through devotion, praying fast but shallow, singing much but absorbing little. We take in spiritual air too quickly to be transformed by it.
- **Suffocation** happens when we stop breathing altogether, when prayer feels forced, worship feels stale, and we convince ourselves we're "just tired," while our spirit's oxygen levels are dropping.

When the Church loses its rhythm of inhale and exhale, everything becomes labored. Ministry becomes motion without meaning. Leaders burn out. Members check out. And what should feel like breathing begins to feel like asthma in the Spirit, every attempt to connect to God feels tight, restricted, forced.

Ezekiel saw this firsthand in the valley of dry bones (**Ezekiel 37**). The bodies were assembled, bones, sinews, and flesh, but they weren't alive until the breath of God entered them. The Body of Christ today looks similar, structure, order, and systems in place, but no wind moving through the lungs of worship. We can have excellent programs and still lack pulse if we lose the breath of the Spirit. Worship isn't supposed to be a song we sing for God; it's the breath we share with Him.

Faith Prescription: Heaven's Oxygen Protocol

1. **Practice Spiritual Breathing:** Start your mornings by inhaling God's Word slowly and exhaling yesterday's worry. Literally say, "God, I receive Your peace" as you breathe in and "I release my control" as you breathe out.

2. **Avoid Contaminated Air:** Stop inhaling the smog of social comparison, negativity, and religious performance. Your lungs weren't made to breathe in approval or applause.

3. **Relearn Stillness:** Oxygen exchange happens best when you're calm. You can't inhale revelation while hyperventilating with anxiety. Create daily moments where silence becomes sacred oxygen.

4. **Sing Until You Mean It:** Worship doesn't need perfect pitch; it needs honest exhale. Let praise unclog your lungs and humility fill them again.

5. **Check Your Spiritual Capacity:** How long can you stay in God's presence before you get restless? If the answer is "not long," your lungs need conditioning. The longer you stay, the stronger you breathe.

Side effects may include renewed joy, spontaneous singing, and a noticeable peace that replaces panic.

Holy Spirit Consult

Doctor's Note: You're breathing, but barely. You've mistaken adrenaline for oxygen. You worship to survive moments instead of to sustain life. I am the breath that animates your faith, the wind that fills your lungs with endurance. You keep holding your breath waiting for clarity, but freedom only comes when you exhale control. Stop gasping through spiritual anxiety. Just breathe Me in again." The Holy Spirit doesn't demand a show; He responds to surrender. He's not impressed by the length of your song, but by the rhythm of your breathing. Let Him refill your lungs with living air until worship feels less like a task and more like oxygen therapy.

Guided Prayer

*"**Breath of Life,** I confess that I've been gasping instead of resting. I've tried to hold my breath through fear, control, and exhaustion. Today I open my lungs to You again. Inhale Your peace. Exhale my panic. Inhale Your presence. Exhale my pride. Teach me to breathe in Your Word and breathe out Your will until worship becomes*

natural again. Fill me with fresh air, not hype, but holy stillness, and let everything in me that has breath praise You. In Jesus 'name, amen."

Reflection Page

1. When was the last time you truly felt the "breath" of God, not emotionally, but deeply?

____

____

____

2. What situations make your spirit feel short of breath? What could be clogging your capacity to worship freely?

____

____

____

____

3. Are you inhaling more fear than faith? What would it look like to reverse that rhythm this week?

____

____

____

____

4. How can you create space for silence without panicking in the stillness?

____

____

____

5. If worship is the Church's respiratory system, what role do you play in keeping the air pure, encourager, intercessor, or purifier of gossip-filled rooms?

____

____

____

Diagnostic Reminder: Don't confuse hype with air. God's presence is not a performance to attend; it's oxygen to live on.

Reflections

____

____

____

____

____

____

Chapter 3:

Nerve Damage, When The Body Stops Responding To The Head

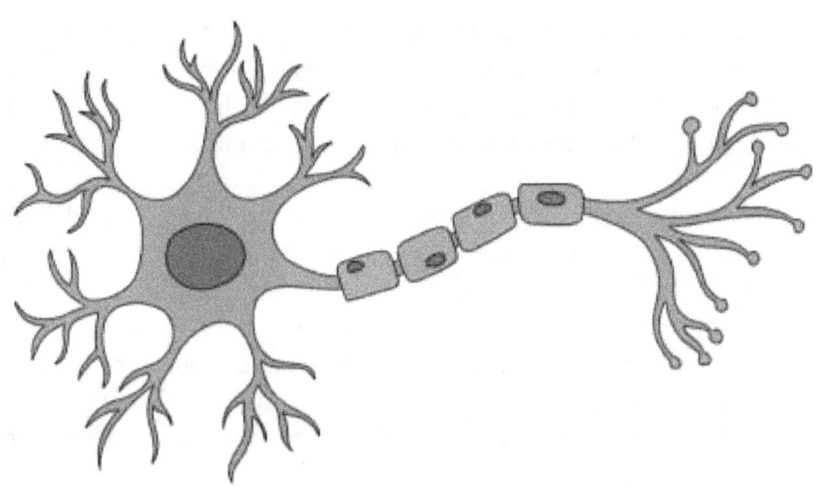

SYMPTOM: Spiritual Paralysis And Numbness

Somewhere between the noise of ministry and the pressure to perform, the Church has developed a case of spiritual nerve damage. We hear sermons, but they no longer move us. We feel conviction, but delay obedience. We say we're "led by the Spirit," but truthfully, we're led by schedules, platforms, and personal logic. When a person's nervous system stops communicating with their brain, the body either freezes or spasms, paralyzed in one area and overreacts in another.

That's exactly what happens in the spiritual Body of Christ when the members stop responding to the Head, Jesus. Some believers can't move forward in faith (spiritual paralysis), while others overreact emotionally without divine instruction (spiritual spasm).

It's not rebellion at first; it's just delayed response. But delayed obedience is still disobedience. The Church doesn't need more movement, it needs connection. Because motion without communication is chaos. And too often, we're mistaking noise for nervous system activity. We have believers functioning on reflexes reacting to trends, emotions, and offense, while ignoring the signals from Heaven. The result? A body that twitches for attention but never truly moves in purpose.

TEACHING:
The Nervous System Of The Kingdom

Your nervous system is the communication highway between the brain and every cell. It translates thoughts into movement, commands into coordination. When your nerves are healthy, every signal gets through; when they're damaged, the message gets distorted.

Spiritually, Jesus Christ is the Head, and the Holy Spirit functions as the nervous system, transmitting divine signals to every member of His Body. When the Church is connected, it moves with fluid grace and synchronized purpose. But when communication is disrupted by pride, fear, or distraction, spiritual reflexes malfunction.

Paul described this clearly in Ephesians 4:15–16: *"We will grow to become in every respect the mature body of him who is the head, that is, Christ. From him the whole body... grows and builds itself up in love, as each part does its work."* That is a picture of healthy neurology, sensitivity, coordination, and unity. But look at what's happening today: the Church has become numb to conviction and hypersensitive to criticism. We've lost touch with the Head. We still "move" programs, plans, and posts, but without direction, those movements aren't ministry; they're spasms of self-importance.

In the natural body, nerve damage often starts small, a little numbness, a tingling you can ignore, until suddenly, you can't feel what's hurting you anymore. Spiritually, that's when sin becomes manageable, correction feels optional, and silence from God doesn't bother you. You're not fine; you're desensitized.

The Church must relearn how to *feel* again, not emotionally, but spiritually. That means sensing God's whisper before He must shout, responding to conviction before He must confront. Because a disconnected nerve doesn't just lose sensitivity, it also loses coordination with the rest of the body. That is why disunity in the Church often starts with desensitized individuals.

When believers can no longer feel what the Head feels, His compassion, His grief, His direction, the whole Body becomes uncoordinated. Hands reaching where He never pointed. Feet running where He never sent. Lips speaking what He never said. The issue isn't bad intention, it's broken connection.

Faith Prescription: Restoring Sensitivity and Response

1. **Spiritual Neuropathy Test:** Pause daily and ask, "Did I feel God's prompting today, or did I just do what felt right?" Desensitization starts with self-direction.
2. **Limit Noise Exposure:** Every nerve needs recovery. Reduce spiritual overstimulation, too many voices, podcasts, or preachers can drown out the Head's signal.

3. **Rebuild Communication Pathways:** Spend intentional time in silence, asking the Holy Spirit to recalibrate your response time. Immediate obedience restores connection.

4. **Apply Reflex Therapy:** Practice instant response to small nudges. Text the person God suggests. Apologize quickly. Pray when you feel the urge. Quick obedience strengthens sensitivity.

5. **Cut Spiritual Caffeine:** Emotional hype can mimic divine instruction. Don't confuse adrenaline for anointing. Learn to discern God's calm, not just His fire.

Side effects may include sharper discernment, conviction clarity, and renewed alignment with God's timing.

Holy Spirit Consult

Doctor's Note: Your nerves are still there, but they're not responding to Me as quickly as they used to. You've trained yourself to react to notifications faster than revelation. I send signals, but you delay them under the weight of logic. I whisper correction, but you buffer it through pride. I don't need your movement; I need your sensitivity. The Body can't follow a Head it refuses to feel." "Stay connected.

Every miracle, every message, every mission begins as a signal from the Head. Be still enough to sense it and surrendered enough to follow it." The Holy Spirit isn't just a power source, He is the **synapse of Heaven**, connecting divine thought to earthly obedience. When you stay in tune with His impulses, you won't just move for God, you'll move *with* Him.

Guided Prayer

"Father, the true Head of my life, I repent for every time I've moved without Your instruction. I confess I've allowed busyness to drown out Your gentle signals. Rewire my spiritual nerves. Restore sensitivity where I've grown numb. Teach me to feel Your heartbeat before I act, To sense Your presence before I speak, To obey instantly when You call. Let my movements match Your mind, and my reflexes mirror Your will. May I never become comfortable with silence that isn't peace. But instead stay responsive to Your whisper. In Jesus' name, amen."

Reflection Page

6.   When was the last time you sensed God's direction, and obeyed immediately? What happened as a result?

____

____

____

7.   Where in your life have you grown "numb" to conviction, an area you no longer feel challenged in?

____

____

____

8. Do you tend to move impulsively (without confirmation) or freeze in fear (delayed obedience)?

____

____

____

9. How can you practice daily sensitivity, small acts of instant obedience that keep you connected to the Head?

____

____

____

10. What relationships or habits might be interfering with the signals from Heaven?

____

____

____

____

____

____

Diagnostic Reminder: Sensitivity is sacred. The moment you stop feeling, you stop following. The Great Physician can restore your reflexes, but you must stay on the table long enough for the rewiring.

Chapter 4:

Spineless Faith: When The Church Loses Its Backbone

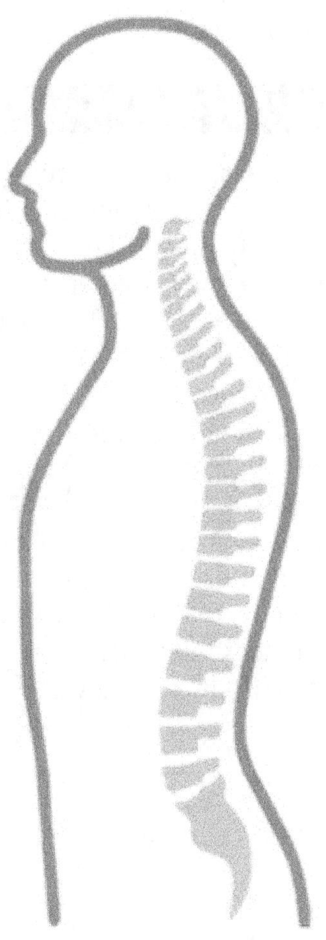

SYMPTOM: Posture Problems In The Spirit

Somewhere between "God understands me" and "Don't judge me," the Church slipped a disc. Conviction has turned into chronic back pain: we can't stand tall in truth without wincing from people's opinions. 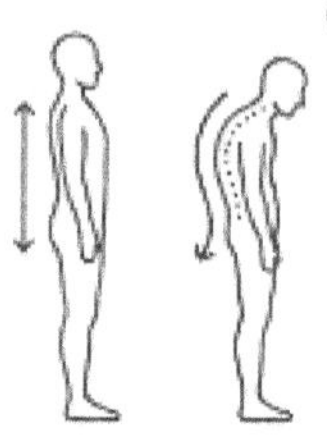The Body still looks impressive on Sundays, but inside the frame is soft cartilage where bone should be. You know the signs of **spineless faith**: doctrines bent to fit comfort, believers folding under culture's weight, and leaders more flexible than faithful. A healthy spine holds a body upright; a weak one bows to pressure.

TEACHING: The Framework Of Faith

The skeletal system gives shape and protection. It keeps the body aligned so muscles, nerves, and organs can function. Spiritually, doctrine and conviction do the same thing. They give form to grace and guard the heart from collapse. When a person's spine curves unnaturally, it's called **scoliosis**; when a believer's convictions curve to match convenience, it's the same disorder in the soul. Paul wrote, *"Stand firm and hold fast to the teachings we passed on to you."* (2 Thessalonians 2 :15). That word *stand* implies resistance, not aggression, but stability.

The early Church carried solid bone. They broke bread in unity, endured persecution, and refused to compromise truth for popularity. Today, we prefer comfort orthopedics: flexible theology, soft sermons, and padded correction. But a Body that never builds bone density eventually becomes brittle. 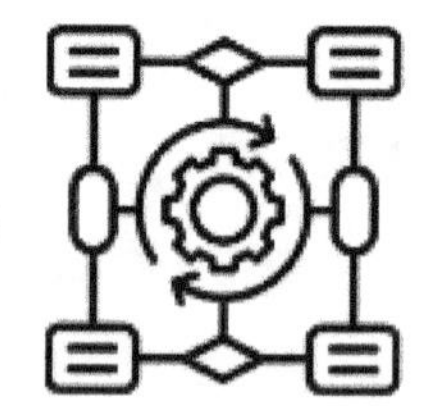

Without doctrine, every emotional trend knocks us over; without conviction, we bend until we break. God designed faith with structure:

- **The spine** - truth that anchors us.

- **The rib - boundaries** that guard our heart.
- **The joints** - humility that allows movement without dislocation.

If the Body of Christ is collapsing, it isn't from lack of passion, it's from lack of posture.

Faith Prescription: Heaven's Orthopedic Plan

1. **Calcium of Conviction:** Take one dose of Scripture before every decision. Strength grows from consistency, not convenience.

2. **Stretch in Grace:** Truth without tenderness causes stiffness; grace without truth causes slouching. Stretch both daily.

3. **Strength Training:** Practice standing firm in small things, integrity at work, honesty in speech, purity in private. Every repetition builds backbone.

4. **Correct Posture:** Check alignment with the Word, not with opinion polls. If something feels "off," return to the plumb line of Scripture.

5. **Rest and Repair:** Bones rebuild during rest. Sabbath isn't laziness; it's how spiritual structure regenerates.

Side effects may include holy confidence, reduced people-pleasing, and unapologetic truth spoken in love.

Holy Spirit Consult

Doctor's Note: Your X-ray shows micro-fractures, small compromises that looked harmless until they multiplied. You've been bending to stay liked when I called you to stand to be light. Real love sometimes stands straight while the world slouches. Let Me reset the bones; it will hurt, but you'll walk upright again." The Spirit's adjustments are never punishment, their posture correction. Each crack you hear is a lie leaving alignment.

"God of Truth and Structure," I've gone limp where I should have stood tall. Forgive the times I traded backbone for approval. Straighten my spine with Your Word. Strengthen my frame with courage. Let integrity be my posture and humility my movement. When culture leans, it helps me remain upright, not stiff with pride but sturdy with purpose. Keep me aligned with Christ, the Cornerstone. In Jesus 'name, amen."

1. Where have you been bending truth to keep peace or avoid conflict?

____

____

____

2. What doctrines or values once felt solid but have softened under pressure?

____

____

____

3. How can you strengthen your "core" the disciplines that keep you upright?

---

4.   Who in your life models good spiritual posture? What can you learn from them?

---

5.   When the next cultural storm blows, will your spine hold or sway? Plan your stance now.

Diagnostic Reminder: A flexible spine is healthy; a spineless one is deadly. Stand straight in truth so the rest of the Body can move freely.

PERSONAL NOTES

46

Chapter 5:

Malnourished Members: When The Church Stops Digesting The Word

SYMPTOM: Overfed But Under-Nourished

The average believer today has access to more spiritual food than any generation before: podcasts, devotionals, live streams, conferences, reels, and inspirational quotes every five seconds. Yet somehow, we're starving. The signs are obvious, spiritual fatigue, shallow endurance, chronic craving for affirmation, and an inability to stand when storms hit. We have plenty of intake but very little digestion. The Body is bloated with information and constipated with application.

We call it "being fed," but being fed and being **nourished** are not the same. A baby can drink all day and still cry if it never learns to swallow. The Church has become full but fragile, stuffed with sermons, starving for substance.

TEACHING: The Digestive System Of The Spirit

In the natural body, digestion is about transformation: breaking food down so nutrients can be absorbed and distributed. Your stomach isn't just a storage room; it's a laboratory. Spiritually, the Word of God works the same way. Reading it isn't enough; it must be **processed**. Meditation breaks it down; obedience absorbs it; endurance distributes its energy to the rest of your life. When digestion fails, the body either stores waste or starves its cells. When spiritual digestion fails, believers either hoard revelation without action or reject conviction because it's uncomfortable. James warned us plainly: *"Do not merely listen to the word and so deceive yourselves. Do what it says."* (**James 1:22**)

Every sermon you hear should be metabolized into movement. Every verse you read should become vitamin strength for your spirit.

But we keep nibbling at Scripture like snacks, never chewing long enough for transformation.

The digestive system of the Church was designed to:

- **Ingest Truth:** Regular exposure to Scripture.
- **Break It Down:** Reflect, question, and let conviction soften hard spots.
- **Absorb Nutrients:** Apply what you've learned to real behavior.
- **Eliminate Waste:** Release lies, guilt, and worldly toxins that no longer serve you.

When any step is skipped, the whole Body feels sluggish. Energy drops. Ministry slows. Unity cramps. We start reaching for spiritual junk food, catchy clichés, emotional heights, anything quick that fills the emptiness. The Word isn't fast food; it's living bread. Jesus said, *"My food is to do the will of Him who sent Me."* (John 4:34) Notice that, **to do**, not just to read.

Faith Prescription: Heaven's Nutritional Plan

1. **Chew Slowly:** Read small portions of Scripture and sit with them. Ask, "What does this reveal about God and what must change in me?" Reflection is spiritual mastication.

2. **Avoid Sugar Substitutes:** Not every "Christian" message is wholesome. Filter teachings through Scripture's ingredient label. If it feeds ego, not humility, it's empty calories.

3. **Stay Hydrated in the Spirit:** The digestive tract of faith needs the water of the Word (Eph 5:26). Dehydrated believers can't process revelation.

4. **Detox Regularly:** Confession clears toxins of guilt and pride that block nutrient flow. Don't let old offense ferment.

5. **Exercise What You Eat:** Serve, give, forgive, lead, turn intake into output. Muscles of faith grow only through motion.

Follow this regimen consistently. Expect improved energy in prayer life, better spiritual metabolism, and a noticeable glow of gratitude.

Holy Spirit Consult

Doctor's Note: "Your stomach is full of unprocessed sermons. You've been swallowing truth but spitting out conviction. I'm not sending new revelation until you digest the last prescription. Chew what I've already given you; obedience releases nutrients that information never will. When the Word becomes flesh in your life, the whole Body will gain strength again." The Spirit's tone isn't shaming; it's restorative. Heaven would rather have a Church that lives one verse well than memorizes a thousand and digests none.

Guided Prayer

"Bread of Heaven, I admit I've been grazing on Your Word without truly eating. I've swallowed promises but skipped obedience. Feed me again, slowly, deeply. Teach me to meditate until truth becomes part of me. Let Your Word burn away every toxin of pride and doubt. Help me crave substance, not sensation. Make me a doer who digests, not a hearer who hoards. In Jesus' name, amen."

Reflection Page

1.   What "spiritual foods" fill your schedule but leave you hungry?

____

____

____

____

2.   Which recent Work from God have you avoided "digesting" because it required change?

____

____

____

____

3.   How can you practice chewing, slowing down, journaling, or discussing Scripture before moving on?

____

____

____

____

4.   What toxins (unforgiveness, shame, negativity) need to be released for healthy digestion?

____

____

____

____

____

5. Record a moment when applying the Word gives you unexpected strength. What spiritual nutrients did it release?

____

____

____

____

Diagnostic Reminder: Information without transformation causes indigestion. The Word only nourishes when it's swallowed, digested, and lived.

Reflections

____

____

____

____

____

____

____

____

____

Chapter 6:

The Immune System Malfunction, When Discernment Stops Working

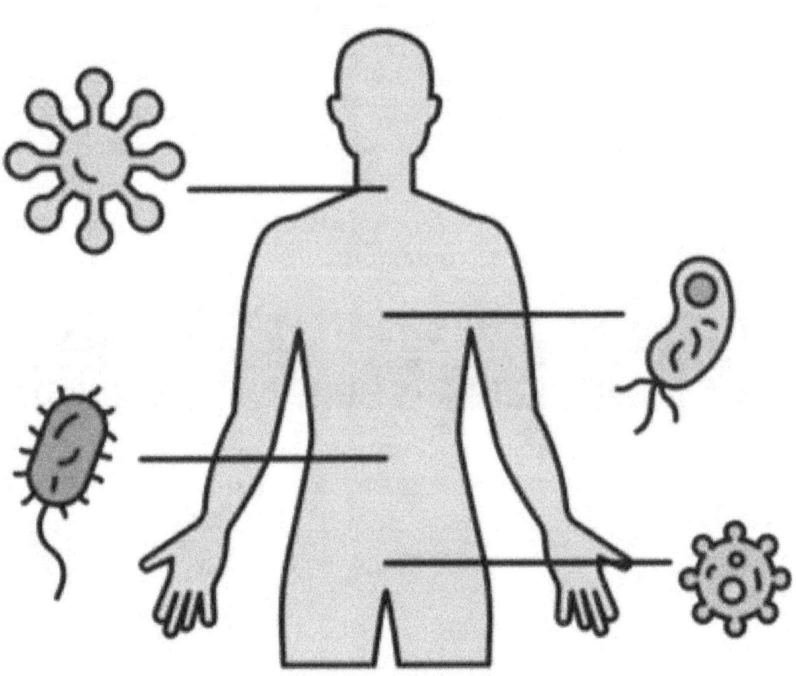

SYMPTOM: Contaminated Faith And Compromised Discernment

It starts small, a catchy phrase that sounds biblical but isn't, a message that flatters more than it convicts, a spiritual leader who substitutes charisma for character. First, you don't think much of it. You even share it. But then confusion spreads. You start doubting what's true. You can't tell conviction from condemnation, truth from trend, Spirit from self.

 Congratulations, your immune system is down. The Body of Christ has been sneezing out hype and coughing up compromise for years because its spiritual antibodies, discernment, accountability, and truth testing, are dangerously low. False teaching, emotional manipulation, and religious extremism spread like viruses through an unprotected Church. People are chasing goosebumps instead of God, sharing reels instead of revelation, and mistaking crowd energy for divine confirmation. When discernment fails, deception feels like destiny. And infection doesn't just make the Church sick; it makes her contagious.

TEACHING:
The Immune System Of The Kingdom

Your immune system's job is simple: recognize what belongs and attack what doesn't. It identifies harmful invaders and produces antibodies to protect the body from disease. When it's healthy, you recover quickly. When it's weak, even a minor germ becomes life-threatening.

Discernment functions the same way in the Body of Christ. It's the Holy Spirit's immune response, the ability to **test the spirits (1 John 4:1)** and identify what's holy versus what's harmful.

But the Church has been living on spiritual antibiotics, constantly reacting to infections we could've prevented if we'd built stronger immunity in the Word.

Discernment weakens when:

- **Emotion replaces examination.** We "feel" everything but verify nothing.
- **Entertainment replaces edification.** We'd rather be impressed than instructed.
- **Popularity replaces purity.** We trust influence more than intimacy with God.

A healthy immune system doesn't attack the body itself. Likewise, discernment isn't suspicion or gossip; its truth wrapped in love. Paul said in Philippians 1:9–10, *"I pray that your love may abound more and more in knowledge and depth of insight, so that you may be able to discern what is best."*

Love and discernment work together. When love stops, discernment mutates into judgment; when discernment stops, love becomes gullible. The Body of Christ can't afford spiritual autoimmunity, believers attacking one another while ignoring the real enemy. We're not called to bite each other; we're called to build antibodies against deception. And that starts by strengthening discernment through truth intake, spiritual maturity, and accountability.

Faith Prescription: Heaven's Immunity Protocol

1. **Daily Truth Supplements:** Read Scripture before you scroll. The Word trains your spiritual immune system to recognize lies faster.

2. **Stop Sharing Every Prophetic Meme:** Test before you repost. Ask: "Does this align with the nature of Jesus and the authority of Scripture?"

3. **Practice Healthy Exposure:** Don't isolate from correction or differing perspectives, they strengthen discernment like vaccines strengthen immunity.

4. **Stay Hydrated with Humility:** Pride weakens defense. A humble heart hears God clearly.

5. **Build Community Immunity:** Stay connected to mature believers who can help identify unhealthy teaching or toxic patterns you've grown used to. Side effects may include clearer thinking, reduced confusion, and a sudden allergy to counterfeit gospels.

Holy Spirit Consult

Doctor's Note: "You've been taking supplements from too many sources. Your system can't tell poison from protein. You swallow anything labeled 'Christian 'without checking the ingredients. I'm calling you to detox, less noise, more Word. Let Me rebuild your immune system through truth that's tested, not trendy. Discernment is not suspicion; it's intimacy with Me." The Holy Spirit isn't trying to make you skeptical; He's trying to make you safe. Discernment isn't paranoia; it's protection. When you walk closely with Him, you'll start sensing contamination before it ever reaches your spirit.

Guided Prayer

"Spirit of Truth, I admit I've let too many voices shape my faith. Forgive me for trusting emotions more than Your Word. Strengthen my discernment until I know Your voice above all others. Filter every thought, teaching, and influence through Your truth. Give me wisdom to spot deception early and courage to confront it lovingly. Cleanse me from the infections of pride, fear, and confusion. Restore my spiritual immune system, not skeptical, but sensitive to You. In Jesus 'name, amen."

Reflection Page

1. What "spiritual infections" have weakened your discernment, fear, pride, flattery, or lack of Word intake?

____

____

____

2. When was the last time you tested a message or teaching by Scripture before agreeing with it?

____

____

3. Are you more drawn to messages that comfort you or confront you? What does that reveal about your immune strength?

____

____

4. Who in your life helps you discern truth when you're unsure, and how can you stay accountable to them?

____

____

____

____

____

5.   What does healthy discernment look like in your daily life, at work, online, and in relationships?

____

____

____

____

Diagnostic Reminder: Discernment isn't about suspicion; it's about saturation, filling your system with so much truth that lies can't survive in it.

Reflections

____

____

____

____

____

____

Chapter 7:

Emotional Instability: When The Hormones Of The Body Of Christ Go Haywire

SYMPTOM: Mood Swings In Ministry

One week you're on fire for God; the next, you can barely light a match. One minute you're singing "I surrender all," and the next you're negotiating which parts to keep. The heights of revival and the lows of real life keep trading places, and the Church calls it normal. We've become a body ruled by hormones instead of holiness, a people whose emotions drive their faith instead of faith driving their emotions. Our spiritual hormones fluctuate with attendance, applause, or answered prayers. When things go right, we shout. When they go wrong, we ghost. Emotional instability in the Body of Christ looks like believers who are passionate but unpredictable, worshippers one day and worriers the next. Pastors preaching truth but crashing emotionally after criticism. Saints serve out of overflow one week and resentment the next. We've mistaken adrenaline for anointing, hype for health. The Church isn't having a revival problem; it's having a regulation problem.

TEACHING: The Endocrine System Of The Spirit

The endocrine system is the internal communication network that keeps the body balanced. Hormones regulate growth, energy, and mood. Too much or too little of one chemical, and the body spirals into chaos. Spiritually, this is the work of the **Holy Spirit** through the **Fruit of the Spirit**, love, joy, peace, patience, kindness, goodness, faithfulness, gentleness, and self-control (Galatians 5:22–23).

These are Heaven's hormones, designed to keep your soul balanced no matter what the external environment throws at you. When the Body of Christ ignores these spiritual regulators, mood takes over mission. We become reactionary, rejoicing when things go our way, collapsing when they don't. Emotional inflammation flares up, causing spiritual swelling that distorts judgment. Unchecked anger becomes spiritual cortisol, slowly burning through relationships.

Jealousy spikes like adrenaline, producing envy-induced exhaustion. Fear dumps anxiety hormones that paralyze obedience. God designed emotional expression, not emotional control. Jesus wept. He rejoiced. He groaned in the Spirit. But He never let emotion outrun assignment. A healthy endocrine system doesn't suppress hormones, it regulates them. Likewise, healthy believers don't ignore emotion; they submit it to the Spirit. Romans 8:6 reminds us, *"The mind governed by the flesh is death, but the mind governed by the Spirit is life and peace."* Governed means managed, regulated, kept in rhythm. When the Spirit is in control, emotions become instruments, not idols.

Faith Prescription, Heaven's Emotional Regulation Plan

1. **Check Your Levels Daily:** Before reacting, ask: "Is this emotion Spirit-led or self-fed?" Awareness is spiritual lab work.

2. **Take Peace Supplements:** Memorize and meditate on Philippians 4:6-7. Anxiety decreases as prayer increases.

3. **Maintain a Balanced Diet:** Consume both correction and encouragement. Too much sugar (affirmation) causes emotional crashes.

4. **Hydrate with Humility:** Pride dehydrates peace. Admit it when your emotions are louder than your obedience.

5. **Exercise Self-Control:** Spiritual maturity looks like choosing response over reaction, pause, pray, proceed.

Side effects may include internal calm, reduced spiritual drama, and immunity to emotional manipulation.

Holy Spirit Consult

Doctor's Note: Your levels are fluctuating. Too much fear, not enough faith. Spikes of passion followed by crashes of discouragement. I'm prescribing consistency, daily doses of My Word, rest, and gratitude. Stop riding the roller coaster of feelings and step into the rhythm of peace. I didn't design you to suppress your emotions; I designed you to sanctify them. Let Me regulate what's been reacting." The Spirit doesn't shame emotion, He shepherds it. He teaches the Body to worship without needing a crowd and to trust without needing control.

Guided Prayer

"Holy Regulator, I confess my emotions have led more than they've listened. I've let fear set my pace and frustration fuel my reactions. Today, I surrender my emotional rhythm to You. Regulate my highs and lows with Your peace. Let joy stabilize me when pain tempts me to spiral. Let patience anchor me when impatience wants to perform. Teach me to feel deeply but follow faithfully. Balance me from the inside out, until the Fruit of Your Spirit becomes my normal state of being. In Jesus 'name, amen."

Reflection Page

1. Which emotions dominate your faith walk, fear, anger, excitement, or doubt?

____

____

____

2. When was the last time you paused before reacting and invited the Spirit to regulate your response?

____

____

____

3. Do you crave emotional highs in worship, or are you learning to value consistent peace?

____

____

____

4. How can you practice "emotional tithing" giving God your first reaction before giving anyone else your response?

____

____

____

5. What habits could help you stabilize spiritually, prayer rhythm, healthy rest, or surrounding yourself with grounded believers?

____

____

____

____

____

Diagnostic Reminder: The goal isn't to feel nothing, it's to feel everything through Him. Let the Spirit govern your mood so your mission doesn't depend on it.

PERSONAL NOTES

Chapter 8:

Blood Clots And Blockages: When Unity Gets Stuck

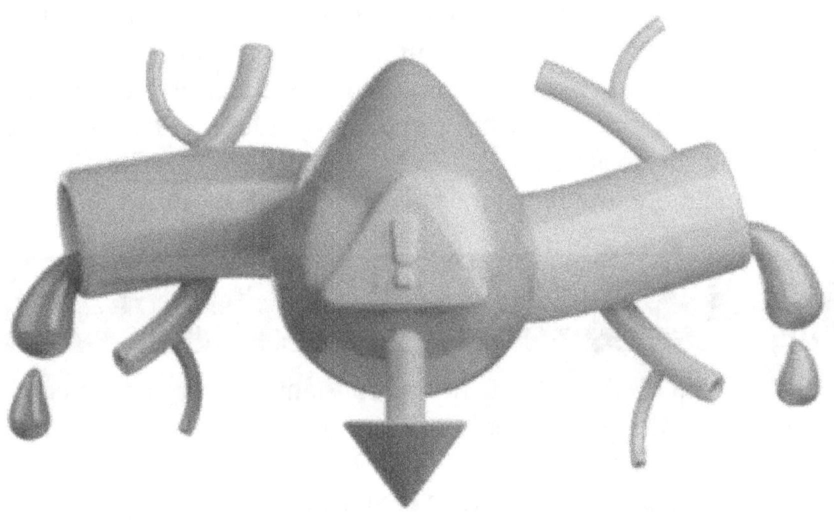

SYMPTOM: The Church Has A Clot

You can always tell when circulation in the Body of Christ has stopped, the warmth of fellowship cools, compassion slows, and what used to feel alive starts feeling numb. Every congregation, every family, every ministry team eventually faces this: a blockage in the flow of grace. It's not that the heart (Jesus) stopped pumping love; it's that the vessels got clogged with offense, ego, and comparison. The problem isn't the source; it is the system.

Blood clots in the Church look like small grudges that grow hard over time. Silent resentments. Petty rivalries. People refusing to talk to one another but still "serving God." It's the worship leader who won't look at the drummer, the prayer team divided by politics, the family who loves Jesus but avoids His people. And here's the most tragic part: when one area is blocked, the entire Body feels it. Ministry slows down. Joy weakness. New believers suffocate under the weight of old wounds. The Church doesn't need more programs; it needs **circulation restoration.**

TEACHING: The Circulatory Network Of The Kingdom

In the human body, blood flows constantly, carrying oxygen, nutrients, and life to every organ. When a clot forms, even a small one, everything downstream is at risk. One tiny blockage can lead to a full-blown stroke or heart attack. Spiritually, unity is that flow. Grace is the blood. And the **Body of Christ** depends on the continual movement of forgiveness, communication, and humility to keep every member alive and healthy.

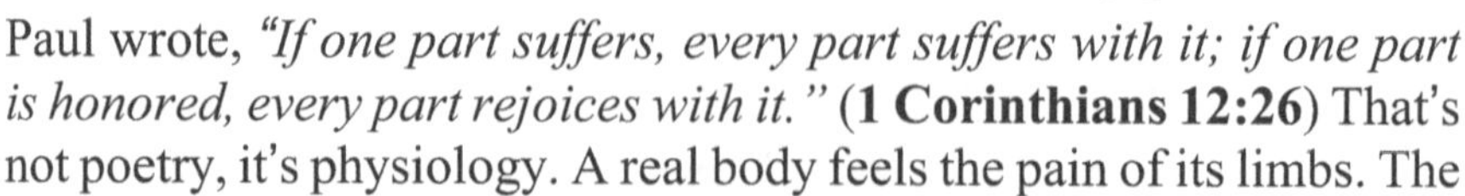

Paul wrote, *"If one part suffers, every part suffers with it; if one part is honored, every part rejoices with it."* (**1 Corinthians 12:26**) That's not poetry, it's physiology. A real body feels the pain of its limbs. The modern Church, however, has developed emotional neuropathy, we've gone numb to each other's suffering. We celebrate in isolation, heal in secret, and bleed quietly while calling it faith. When the Body stops feeling, it stops flowing. When it stops flowing, it starts dying, slowly, silently, symptom by symptom. What causes the blockages?

- **Offense:** hardened plaque that restricts the flow of grace.
- **Pride:** the cholesterol of the soul, coating every good work with self-glory.
- **Unforgiveness:** sticky buildup that keeps bitterness circulating.
- **Division:** severed vessels that no longer communicate with the heart.

The Church's immune response should be reconciliated. But we keep applying band aids of politeness over infected wounds of disunity. Jesus was clear in John 13:35, *"By this everyone will know that you are my disciples, if you love one another."* Not by how well we preach, sing, or post, but by how well we **flow together.** Unity isn't uniformity, it's cooperation.It's veins, arteries, and capillaries carrying the same life through different paths, serving one Head and one heartbeat.

Faith Prescription, Heaven's Circulation Restoration Plan

1. **Cardiac Rehab Through Reconciliation:** Identify one relationship where the flow has stopped. Write a message, make a call, or extend a hand, not for closure, but for cleansing.

2. **Forgiveness Transfusion:** Stop recycling offense. The more you replay it, the thicker the blood gets. Release it before it poisons the rest of your system.

3. **Keep Movement in the Body:** Isolation causes clotting. Stay active in community even when connection feels inconvenient.

4. **Take the Anticoagulant of Humility:** Pride clots faster than sin; humility thins the blood so grace can flow freely.

5. **Stay Hydrated with Gratitude:** Thank God daily for other members of the Body, especially the ones who stretch your patience. Gratitude keeps love liquid.

Side effects may include spontaneous forgiveness, unexpected peace, and restored friendships that only grace could explain.

Holy Spirit Consult

Doctor's Note: Your circulation report shows multiple blockages: resentment in your leadership arteries, pride in your personal veins, and fatigue in your fellowship capillaries. You've been functioning on bypass mode, doing ministry without connection. I can restore the flow, but you must consent to the surgery of reconciliation. Unity is not optional; it's oxygen." I'm calling you to become a transfusion center, not waiting for grace to reach you but letting grace flow through you. When My love moves freely between members, the whole-Body glows with life again." The Holy Spirit doesn't just repair vessels, He reopens hearts. When you allow Him to dissolve the clots of offense, the warmth of community returns, and spiritual color floods back into pale places.

Guided Prayer

"Heavenly Cardiologist, I've carried grudges like blockages. I've let pride thicken the flow of grace in my heart. Today, I surrender to Your circulation plan. Clear out every place where bitterness built up. Let Your love flow through me to others, freely, fully, faithfully. Teach me to forgive quickly, reconcile courageously, and love consistently. Make me a vessel that never resists Your flow. In Jesus 'name, amen."

Reflection Page

1. Who have you silently resented while pretending to be "at peace"?

____

____

____

2. What conversations or relationships feel blocked, and what step of humility could reopen them?

____

____

____

3. Do you find yourself isolated when offended or staying connected through reconciliation?

____

____

____

4. How does your pride most often clot the flow of grace, defensiveness, gossip, and withdrawal?

____

____

____

____

____

5. What would your church, team, or family look like if unity began circulating again?

____

____

____

Diagnostic Reminder: Revival is not new blood flow, it's restored flow. Keep the veins of fellowship open, and the pulse of love will never stop.

Reflections

____

____

____

____

____

____

____

Chapter 9:

Involuntary Reflexes: When The Body Reacts Before It Prays

SYMPTOM:
The Church's Knee-Jerk Reaction Disorder

We've all been there, moments when our mouth moves faster than our mind, when offense pulls the trigger before the Holy Spirit can whisper, "Wait." The modern believer is reflex-driven: quick to post, quick to argue, quick to quit, and slow to pray.

It is a spiritual disorder that makes the Body of Christ twitch every time it's touched. You can recognize it by the symptoms:
- Defensive reflexes when corrected.
- Emotional flinching when disciplined.
- Snapping responses when misunderstood.
- Reactionary "discernment" that's just suspicion.

When we live by reflex instead of revelation, the result is chaos. Ministries implode from emotional leadership. Relationships fracture from impulsive words. Decisions get made in haste and repented in tears. A healthy spiritual body doesn't react, it responds. Reflexes keep you alive, but responses keep you aligned.

TEACHING: The Reflex System Of The Spirit

In your natural body, reflexes are automatic. They're survival mechanisms, touch something hot, you pull away. Blink when something flies toward your eye. Your body is wired to react before your brain has time to think. But spiritually, growth means learning to pause. When you were an infant in faith, reflexes kept you from danger. But maturity requires discernment, not every discomfort is danger, not every confrontation is cruelty, and not every delay is denial.

The spiritual reflex system works best when synced with the nervous system of obedience (Christ as the Head). The moment you disconnect from the Head, reflex replaces response. That is why Jesus withdrew to pray before reacting (Luke 5:16). His pattern was intentional pause: feeling emotion fully but filtering it through the Father. The Body of Christ often suffers from reaction fatigue, exhausted from fighting battles God never assigned. We respond to every opinion, every online argument, every rumor, every criticism, and by the end of the week, we're bruised from dodging blows that were never ours to take.

Proverbs 29:11 puts it bluntly: *"Fools give full vent to their rage, but the wise bring calm in the end."* Impulse without intercession will always cause injury. God is retraining His Church's reflexes. He's teaching us to breathe before we bite, to worship before we worry, to pray before we post. Because not everything that touches you deserves a twitch.

Faith Prescription, Heaven's Reflex Therapy Plan

1. **Slow Your Reaction Time:** When triggered, take a physical breath and a spiritual one. Inhale truth, exhale assumption.

2. **Run Diagnostics Before Speaking:** Ask: "Is this emotion mine or His?" Sometimes anger is conviction in disguise; other times, it's pride.

3. **Stretch in Stillness:** Build the muscle memory of pause. Spend quiet time daily so silence feels safe, not threatening.

4. **Train Your Reflexes in Worship:** When tension rises, make worship your default response. Praise confuses the enemy and resets your nervous system.

5. **Use the Armor of God as Padding:** Ephesians 6 wasn't poetic; it's practical protection. The shield of faith absorbs hits that once made you flinch

Side effects may include peaceful reactions, longer patience, and the miraculous ability to think before typing.

Holy Spirit Consult

Doctor's Note: Your reflexes are overactive. You jump at offense, jerk at correction, and tense up at truth. You've mistaken reaction for strength. I'm retraining your spiritual body to wait for instruction from the Head before moving. Stillness isn't a weakness, it's stability. Let Me rewire your response system until peace becomes your instinct." The Spirit doesn't remove your reflexes; He sanctifies them. He transforms fight-or-flight into faith-and-flow, so instead of defending yourself, you defer to His direction.

Guided Prayer

"Spirit of Calm Authority, Teach me to pause. Forgive me for reacting from fear, pride, and pain. I've defended myself more than I've depended on You. Rewire my reflexes until I respond like Jesus, slow to anger, quick to listen, steady under pressure. Let patience become my pulse, and prayer become my first movement. Help me to pause, breathe, and obey, not out of fear, but out of trust. In Jesus 'name, amen."

Reflection Page

1. When was the last time you reacted before praying, and what did it cost you?

____

____

____

2.   What triggers make you most defensive, criticism, waiting, or misunderstanding?

____

____

____

3.   How could you start practicing spiritual pauses in your daily life?

____

____

____

____

4.   Who in your circle models Spirit-led response instead of emotional reaction? What can you learn from them?

____

____

____

____

5.   What situation right now requires you to stop twitching and start trusting

____

____

____

____

Diagnostic Reminder: Grode layered how's up in your delay time. The longer you wait before reacting, the quicker heaven can respond on your behalf.

Reflections

____

____

____

____

____

____

____

____

____

____

____

____

Chapter 10:

Vital Signs: Revival Or Resuscitation?

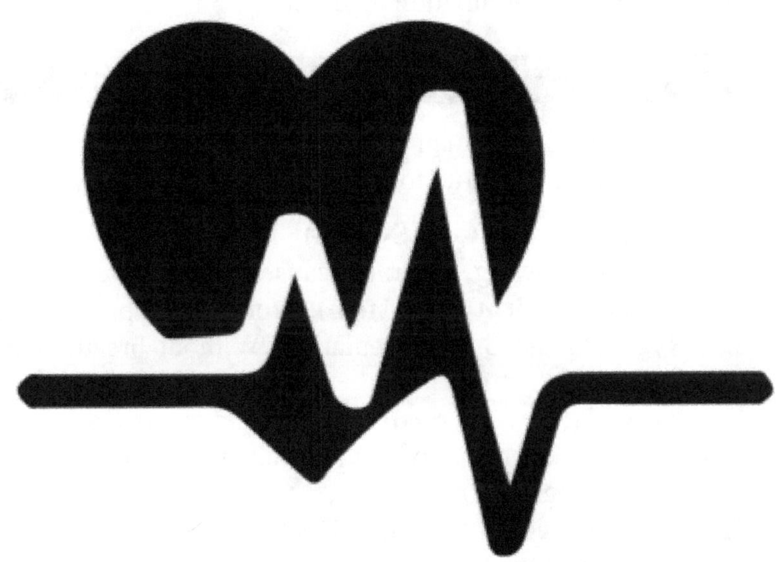

SYMPTOM: Alive But Not Well

The monitors are still beeping, but the movement is minimal. The Body of Christ isn't dead, it's dehydrated. Not unfaithful, but unfocused. Not sick beyond hope but scattered beyond strength. The spiritual charts read like an emergency room board: weak pulse, low oxygen, shallow prayer, high pride, and irregular unity. We sing louder, trying to mask the silence. We host more conferences trying to prove a heartbeat. But if the vital signs are unstable, revival isn't the next event, it's the next breath of repentance. The Church has been living on life support, confusing survival with strength. God's not trying to resuscitate religion; He's restoring relationship. Revival isn't about waking up a dead body; it's about **realigning a living one** that's forgotten how to function together.

TEACHING: The Whole Body In Review

Every system matters. The human body thrives only when its organs operate in sync. The same is true for the spiritual body, the Church.

- **The Heart (Circulatory System)**: Love is the bloodline. When it stops flowing, bitterness causes cardiac arrest.
- **The Lungs (Respiratory System)**: Worship and prayer keep the oxygen of the Spirit circulating. Without breath, faith suffocates.
- **The Nerves (Nervous System)**: Connection to Christ, the Head, ensures coordination. When signals don't reach the limbs, chaos begins.
- **The Bones (Skeletal System)**: Doctrine and integrity hold the Body upright. Without structure, we collapse under cultural weight.
- **The Digestive Tract (Word Processing)**: The Word must be chewed, digested, and applied, not hoarded. Application is nutrition.
- **The Immune System (Discernment)**: Discernment guards' purity. A Body without it becomes infected by falsehood.

- **The Hormones (Endocrine System)**: Emotional stability sustains witness. Spirit regulates what the flesh can't.
- **The Circulatory Network (Unity)**: Connection keeps life flowing. Isolation kills faster than sin.
- **The Reflexes (Response System)**: Delayed obedience and impulsive reactions both disrupt recovery. Prayer steadies' movement.

Each system has been examined. Each diagnosis exposed a spiritual imbalance. And every imbalance points to one core issue, disconnection from the Head. Paul wrote in Ephesians 4:16, *"From Him the whole body, joined and held together by every supporting ligament, grows and builds itself up in love, as each part does its work."* Growth happens only in connection. Revival isn't random fire falling from heaven; it's the result of divine order being restored on earth. God's revival looks less like shouting and more like circulation: love pumping, breath flowing, nerves sensing, bones standing, digestion nourishing, and discernment defending. When every member aligns, the Body doesn't need resuscitation, it lives in perpetual renewal.

Faith Prescription: Heaven's Rehabilitation Plan

1. **Full Alignment Therapy:** Every day, consciously reconnect your will to His. Ask: "Head of the Body, where do You want to move through me today?"

2. **Hydration in the Word:** Dehydration mimics death. Keep drinking Scripture until peace returns to your pulse.

3. **Group Rehab:** Healing happens in community. Stay connected to believers who challenge your comfort and strengthen your stamina.

4. **Heart Rate Monitors:** Evaluate your motives before every ministry act. If it's not love-driven, it's a false rhythm.

5. **Breathing Exercises:** Breathe in grace, exhale control. Pray slowly, deliberate prayers until anxiety's grip weakens.

Side effects may include spiritual clarity, emotional recovery, and increased hunger for unity and holiness.

Holy Spirit Consult

Doctor's Final Note: You're still alive, I can feel the pulse. But you've mistaken adrenaline for anointing, noise for nurture, movement for maturity. I'm not here to revive your calendar; I'm here to resuscitate your communion. The miracle you seek isn't in the crowd, it's in your connection to Me. Stay plugged into the Head, and every system will heal in time." The Body is not dying; it's rediscovering its design. Revival doesn't begin with a shout; it begins with a heartbeat that matches Mine. When the Spirit finishes the exam, He doesn't send you away with prescriptions, He stays as the permanent Physician. Healing in the Kingdom is not a discharge; it's a lifelong relationship with the Doctor.

Guided Prayer

"Great Physician, Thank You for the diagnosis and the mercy that comes with it. I see where my systems have failed and where my spirit has resisted correction. Realign me to the rhythm of Heaven. Let Your Word cleanse me, Your Spirit breathes through me, and Your love circulates within me. Revive every weak place, resuscitate every dead dream, restore every disconnected limb of Your Body. May I never settle for partial healing when wholeness is available. Breathe life back into Your Church until our pulse and Yours are one. In Jesus 'name, amen."

Reflection Page

1. Which system in your spiritual life felt the weakest during this exam, heart, lungs, nerves, bones, digestion, immune, hormones, unity, or reflexes?

____

____

____

2. What daily habits could serve as your "rehabilitation plan" to keep those systems healthy?

____

____

3. How will you stay connected to the Head (Christ) in both stillness and service?

____

____

____

4. What does true revival look like to you now, noise or nourishment, adrenaline or alignment?

____

____

____

5. Record the moment in this journey where you felt God "shock" something back to life. What changed?

____

Diagnostic Reminder: The Great Physician has declared you alive. Healing isn't a one-time miracle; it is a lifelong appointment. Stay connected, stay breathing, and stay in circulation. The Body is healing. The pulse is returning. And revival isn't coming; it's already begun in you.

Reflections

Conclusion

The Patient, The Healer, And The Pulse Of Heaven

You made it. You survived the exam table. You sat through the X-rays of conviction, the MRI of motive, the heart monitor of faith, and the long, uncomfortable silence where the Great Physician said nothing, because sometimes silence *is* surgery. And yet, you're still here. Breathing. Not perfectly, but intentionally. That alone is a miracle.

When you first checked into this Clinic, you probably didn't expect such an invasive inspection. You thought it would be a quick adjustment, maybe a vitamin shot of motivation and a few cute scriptures to tape on your mirror. But the Doctor wasn't after your symptoms; He was after your system. He wanted the root infection, the hidden fracture, the emotional scar tissue that kept you worshiping on autopilot. He wanted you *whole.* And now, after the scans, the tears, and the revelations, you understand what real healing feels like, it's not a rush of power; it's a slow return of peace. It's the sound of your own heartbeat finally syncing with His.

The Moment Everything Changes

The truth is, the Faith Clinic was never just a metaphor. It's your life, your daily walk, your spiritual anatomy lesson, your mirror. Every organ you studied, every diagnosis you faced, was a divine way of saying: "You are My body. You are My patient. You are My instrument." The circulatory system taught you to keep love moving.

The respiratory system reminded you to breathe when life constricts. The nerves reconnected you to the mind of Christ. The skeleton reminded you that truth is non-negotiable. The digestive tract dared you to *do* the Word, not just quote it. The immune system warned you to guard purity and test every spirit. The hormones exposed your moods but returned your balance. The circulatory network showed you the power of reconciliation. The reflexes taught you that delay isn't denial, it's discipline. And finally, the vital signs revealed this: You were never dying. You were evolving.

From Exam To Expression

The Great Physician didn't heal you just so you could *feel* better; He healed you so you could *become* better, for others. Your healed heart is now the clinic someone else needs. Your restored mind is now the medication for another soul. Your story is now a prescription pad, tear off a page and hand it to someone drowning in symptoms you once knew too well. You don't need a platform; you are the platform. You don't need a pulpit; you are the sermon. Every time you choose grace over gossip, every time you breathe peace into panic, every time you forgive instead of flinch, Heaven records it as a miracle performed under your license. This is how revival begins: not with a spotlight, but with circulation. A healed believer walking into a hurting world and letting love move again.

The Final Diagnosis

Your charts are clear. Your vitals are strong. The pulse of Heaven now beats inside you, and the sound is unmistakable life. Not the shallow kind that just exists, but the abundant kind that sings even in suffering. The world is full of patients, but few practitioners. You are both. You know the pain and the prescription. You've lived the diagnosis and survived the treatment. Now, go and keep hearts alive.

The Final Word From The Physician

"Child, I didn't hear you to make you famous. I healed you to make you faithful. I didn't resurrect you for applause; I raised you for assignment. Go. Touch My Body. Teach them to breathe again. Every hand you hold, every word you speak, every tear you wipe, that's Me, still practicing medicine through you."

Reader's Benediction

May your heartbeat never forget who restarted it. May your lungs always inhale grace and exhale truth. May your bones never bow to pressure again. May your mind stay connected to the Head. May your emotions remain balanced by the Spirit. May your discernment detect lies before they infect you. May your words become healing agents, not weapons. May your unity restore circulation in every community you touch. And may your reflex always be prayer, not panic. Because healing isn't a one-time miracle. It's a lifestyle of alignment. It's the steady rhythm of a soul that refuses to flatline again.

Final Prescription

- **Dosage:** One act of love daily.
- **Refills:** Infinite.
- **Side Effects:** Peace, joy, clarity, and the unshakable knowing that you were built to heal.

File Closed: *Faith Clinic, Spiritual Body Exam Complete.*
Status: *Discharged to Serve.*
Condition: *Whole.*
Follow-up: *Daily communion with the Doctor until further notice, or eternity, whichever comes first.* Now go, Practitioner. Keep hearts beating. The Body of Christ is counting on your hands.

The Discharge Summary, You're Healed, But Stay In Follow-Up

(Final Assessment & Release Orders from the Faith Clinic - Spiritual Body Exam)

Patient Name: The Body of Christ
Attending Physician: Dr. Jesus Christ, M.D. - Miracle Distributor

Resident Specialist: The Holy Spirit - Behavioral and Heart Regulation

Admission Reason: Chronic Disconnect, Acute Idolatry, Severe Spiritual Fatigue Status on Discharge: Breathing, Believing, and Finally Listening

Diagnosis Summary

During your stay, several systemic failures were observed:
- **Cardiac Compromise:** Love flow restricted by pride and unforgiveness.

- **Respiratory Weakness:** Worship performed without breath of Spirit.

- **Neurological Delay:** Signals from the Head do not reach the hands and feet.

- **Skeletal Instability:** Backbone of truth softened by people-pleasing.

- **Digestive Malabsorption:** High Word intake, low obedience absorption.

- **Immune Suppression :** Discernment deficient, viral falsehood spread.

- **Hormonal Imbalance:** Faith ruled by feelings instead of fruit.
- **Circulatory Blockage:** Unity obstructed by offense and competition.

- **Reflex Overactivity:** Chronic reaction before prayer syndrome.

Immediate interventions were successful. The Great Physician initiated heart resuscitation through repentance, oxygen therapy through worship, and spinal realignment through truth. Vital signs now read: **stable, responsive, reviving.**

Condition At Discharge

- Pulse of love detectable and steady.
- Respiratory rate (normal praise range) sustained without mechanical assistance.
- Neural pathways between Head and Body reconnected.
- Bone density of conviction increasing.
- Word digestion produces visible fruit of obedience.
- Immune defenses respond rapidly to falsehood.
- Emotional hormones are regulated by peace instead of panic.
- Circulation of grace restored to extremities of the Body.
- Reflex responses slowed to Spirit-led timing.

Discharge Instructions & Follow-Up Care

Continuing Prescribed Medication: Daily Scripture doses (Matthew 4:4), Prayer therapy morning and night (1 Thessalonians 5:17) Worship inhalation as needed (Psalm 150:6)

Dietary Guidelines: Eat solid Word daily; avoid processed opinions. Reduce sugar of flattery; increase fiber of truth. Hydrate with living water (John 7:38).

Activity Restrictions: No heavy lifting of bitterness or offense. Avoid strenuous argument without Spirit clearance. Resume community activity slowly to prevent relapses into isolation.

Therapy Plan: Weekly Body Movement Sessions (aka fellowship). Stretch in grace daily. Strength training through service and forgiveness.

Warning Signs of Relapse: Rapid pulse of anger. Shortness of breath in worship. Numbness to conviction. Loss of appetite for Scripture. Sudden swelling of ego. If any of these symptoms reappear, contact the Holy Spirit immediately. He specializes in after-care and does house calls.

Doctor's Final Remarks

"You came in depleted, dizzy from religious activity without relationship. I've cleaned the wounds, reset the bones, and revived the heart. You're healed, but healing is a habit. Don't leave My presence thinking you no longer need checkups. I am both your Doctor and your Dwelling. Stay close to Me, and you'll stay well." He signs the chart in scarlet ink, blood from Calvary's file.

Discharge Prayer

"**Great Physician,** Thank You for the pain that revealed my condition and the grace that restored my health. Teach me to walk daily in this wholeness. Keep my heart soft, my lungs filled with praise, my mind sensitive to Your signals, my bones strong in truth, and my hands connected to Your Body. Let every system of my life serve Your purpose. I receive Your clearance to live again, not as a survivor, but as a sign of Your healing power. In Jesus 'name, amen."

Follow-Up Appointments

- **Weekly Check-Ins:** Sunday fellowship with the Body.
- **Daily Vitals:** Morning Word and nightly gratitude.
- **Quarterly Exam:** Private retreat with the Physician for re-alignment.

Prognosis: **Excellent, expected to live forever.**

Final Note on Chart: *Patient discharged in stable condition, walking upright, pulse synchronized with Heaven. Recommended lifestyle - love freely, breathe deeply, discern wisely, and stay connected to the Head.*

PERSONAL NOTES

Epilogue:

Released to Heal:
The Doctor Is Now in You

Welcome back into the world, newly discharged and spiritually breathing on your own. You walked into this Clinic gasping, numb, and carrying charts full of excuses. Now look at you, heart steadily, lungs full, eyes clear. The Great Physician has signed your release papers, but He didn't send you home empty-handed. He sent you out carrying His credentials. You are no longer just a **patient** of grace; you are a **practitioner** of it. Everything you endure on the exam table becomes medicine for someone else. The scars you tried to hide are now your spiritual stethoscopes; they help you hear pain in others. The lessons that broke you will now guide you as you help repair what's broken around you.

Your New Role: Kingdom Healer

Every healed believer automatically joins Heaven's medical team.

You are authorized to:

- **Perform Spiritual CPR:** When someone's faith flatlines, speak life, remind them of promises, not problems.

- **Distribute Prescriptions of Peace:** Write hope on hearts the world has written off.

- **Offer Grace Transfusions:** Replace condemnation with compassion everywhere you go.

- **Conduct Routine Checkups:** Ask friends the questions no one else dares, "How's your heart? Are you still breathing in the Spirit?"
- **Teach Preventative Care:** Help new believers build immunity through Scripture, prayer, and community before crisis hits.

You're not replacing the Doctor; you're extending His practice.

Your Uniform

You won't wear scrubs; you'll wear humility. You won't carry a clipboard; you'll carry the cross. Your badge won't say "Dr."; it will read *Servant*. Every time you choose compassion over criticism, you represent the Physician who healed you first.

The Oath Of The Healed

Repeat quietly if you're ready to practice: "I solemnly declare that I will serve as an instrument of the Great Physician. I will examine hearts before judging them, offer truth without arrogance, and administer mercy without favoritism. I will remember that the Body of Christ is one patient, when one member aches, we all attend the wound. I will stay in continuing education through prayer and Word, and I will never claim to heal what only His blood can cure." Congratulations, doctor. You're licensed to love.

Continuing Education Requirements

1. **Case Studies in Compassion**, Study how Jesus healed people others avoided.

2. **Clinical Practice in Forgiveness**, Apply grace daily, especially when it's least deserved.

3. **Emergency Room Experience**, Be present in crisis; ministry often begins in chaos.

4. **Peer Review**, Stay accountable to fellow healers. Pride is malpractice.

5. **Residency in Presence**, Never leave the Physician's side, healing power flows only through proximity.

Doctor's Final Blessing

"Go into all the world and carry My medicine. Lay hands, speak life, forgive freely. Don't hoard the cure, become it. Everywhere your feet step, may healing follow like oxygen."

Parting Prayer

"Great Physician, Thank You for trusting me with Your healing power. Use my voice as comfort, my hands as mercy, my story as proof that You still restore. Keep my spirit tender enough to feel pain but strong enough to help. Wherever I go, let people sense that Heaven has a hospital open inside me. In Jesus 'name, amen."

Prescription For The Road

- Keep your chart open; God's still writing.

- Don't fear new symptoms, their opportunities for deeper healing.

- Remember: revival isn't a conference; it is a lifestyle of continual checkups.

- Stay close to the Head, breathe deeply, and keep the Body alive.

Status: Cleared for active duty in Kingdom medicine. **Next appointment:** The moment someone near your whispers, "I'm not okay." That's your cue, smile gently, roll up your sleeves, and say, **"Welcome to the Clinic."**

Faith Clinic Practitioner's License & Id Card

Issued by Heaven's Department of Healing and Spiritual Restoration

License Type:
Faith Clinic Practitioner - Mental/Emotional Edition - Spiritual Body Exam Certified

Issuing Authority: The Great Physician, Jesus Christ, M.D. (Miracle Distributor)
Authorized by the Holy Spirit (Resident Instructor)
Registration No.: ______________________________
(*Written in Lamb's Book of Life*)

License Holder:______________________________
(*Full Name - as Heaven calls you, not what the world labeled you*)

Date of Commissioning: ______________________________
(*The day you decide to live healed and help others do the same*)

License Classifications:
☑ Emotional First Responder - specializes in spiritual triage for broken hearts.

☑ Soul Surgeon - uses truth as a scalpel and grace as anesthesia.

☑ Compassion Counselor - prescribes prayer, patience, and Scripture therapy.

☑ Revival Nurse - checks pulses and monitors spiritual vitals of the Body.

☑ Unity Technician - repairs relational fractures and circulatory blockages.

Authorized Treatments:
- Administering grace through spoken encouragement.
- Performing spiritual CPR on fainting faith.
- Applying pressure to stop the bleeding of bitterness.
- Writing prescriptions of forgiveness.
- Administering transfusions of love and hope.
- Monitoring vital signs of joy, peace, and humility.

Scope of Practice: Operated only under the supervision of the Holy Spirit. All procedures must be performed in love (1 Corinthians 16:14). Failure to consult the Great Physician before major decisions constitute spiritual malpractice.

License Expiration:
Never. (John 10:28 - Eternal coverage guaranteed.)

Renewal Process:
Daily prayer, weekly fellowship, continual surrender, periodic repentance.

Practitioner's Oath (Signature Required): "I solemnly acknowledge that I am a healed healer, a vessel, not the source; a nurse, not the Physician. I will serve with humility, love with courage, and minister with both compassion and conviction. I will examine myself before diagnosing others, and I will live in such a way that my life proves the Great Physician still makes house calls."
Signature: ____
Date: _______________________________

Identification Details (Back Of ID Card)

Name:_______________________________________

Title: Faith Clinic Practitioner – Authorized Healer

Department: Kingdom Health & Restoration

 Emergency Contact: The Holy Spirit (Available 24/7)

Insurance Coverage: Grace Unlimited - Prepaid in Blood (Romans 5:20)

Specialization Areas:_________________________________

 (*Example: Anxiety, Anger, Grief, Leadership Burnout, Church Hurt, etc.*)

Favorite Healing Scripture: ______________________________

Official Use Only

Seal of Heaven: *Applied at Calvary.*

Verification Contact: *Call on the name of the Lord (Jeremiah 33:3).*

Doctor's Endorsement

"Approved and commissioned for fieldwork. Show mercy boldly. Handle hearts gently. This license is permanent - once healed, forever useful. Signed, **The Great Physician** "

Display Instructions

Keep this license visible - in your Bible, journal, or mirror - as a daily reminder: You are authorized to heal. You are cleared up to love. You are Heaven's practitioner on earth.

PERSONAL NOTES

ABOUT THE AUTHOR

Dr. Patricia Tanner was born and raised in Sanford FL. She comes from a family of three siblings. Patricia Tanner is the founder of Multhai International Realty, Multhai Asset Management Services, and Multhai Investment Group which is located in Sanford, Florida. She is a graduate of the University of Central Florida, where she received a Bachelor of Science in Business Administration and a minor in Human Resources Management.

Dr. Tanner began her career shortly thereafter as a Regional Property Manager in the apartment community. Throughout her career in property management, she has built interpersonal relationships with corporate clients. She has a successful track record of increasing company revenues over $5 million annually, through hard work, commitment, creativeness, and strategic planning.

Her experience and leadership role eventually led her to achieve a Florida Real Estate Broker license. She spent fifteen years in the Real Estate field while completing a Master of Arts in Human Resources Management from Webster University, and a Master of Public Administration from Troy University. It was in this capacity that she decided to open her own brokerage company, Multhai International Realty.

In addition, Dr. Tanner finds time in her busy schedule to participate in her own Non-For-Profit Organization, Stones 2 Homes. She remains President of her organization in which she helps people build, keep, or purchase homes in affordable communities. She is the founder of PNT Property Partners in which she buys vacant land, develops it, and constructs brand new construction homes in Sanford Florida. Her overall goal is to educate and provide resources to help people overcome financial hardships and credit disadvantage to live the American Dream through homeownership in spite of economic hardship. Through her visions she will continue to grow as an entrepreneur and is willing to share her knowledge, experience, and expertise with anyone who is willing to learn.

MORE BOOKS BY THE AUTHOR

Welcome to the Faith Clinic—where your soul doesn't need to be perfect to be healed.

You've smiled through burnout. Quoted scripture while quietly unraveling. Prayed, fasted, and still felt like your faith flatlined. If that's you, Faith Clinic: Volume I is your spiritual prescription.

Dr. Patricia S. Tanner—known as The Faith Doctor—invites you into a raw, grace-filled recovery journey for the soul. With 7 powerful doses of faith-infused wisdom, this book delivers healing where performance failed and offers truth where church hurt left a scar. Designed especially for spiritually exhausted youth and young adults, each "dose" reads like an IV drip of hope for believers secretly running on empty.

You don't need to be okay to show up. You just need to be willing. The clinic is open.

NOW AVAILABLE:
www.amazon.com

Healing was just the beginning. Now it's time to grow.

If Faith Clinic Volume I met you in crisis, Volume II meets you in recovery. Because faith isn't a one-time fix—it's a lifestyle that needs maintenance, accountability, and consistency. Welcome to your follow-up care plan.

In Faith Clinic: Volume II, Dr. Patricia S. Tanner—aka The Faith Doctor—guides you through the next level of your spiritual healing journey. From navigating church trauma and burnout to facing silence from God and rediscovering purpose, this book goes deeper than devotionals. It's not about hype—it's about habits that sustain real, lasting transformation.

With raw wisdom, relatable stories, and no-shame truths, each chapter is a spiritual check-in for believers who want to thrive—not just survive. Whether you're wrestling with doubt, craving stability, or simply ready to grow up in God, this clinic is for you.

You've detoxed. Now it's time to build. Let's get you discharge-ready.

NOW AVAILABLE:
www.amazon.com

Welcome to the Faith Clinic: Anxiety Edition — where God doesn't coddle your coping mechanisms but confronts them with surgical precision.

This book is for the ones who love Jesus but still can't sleep. For the worship leaders crying in church bathrooms. For the believers who pray in spirals, fight shame on Sundays, and secretly think, "Maybe I'm the only one who can't seem to breathe through this." You're not crazy. You're just in a fight — and this book is your spiritual triage.

Inside you'll find:
- Panic attacks in pews and the prayers that still work.
- Scriptures that talk you off the ledge.
- What to do when you feel numb and God feels quiet.
- How to walk out of shame loops, judgment spirals, and performance religion.

This isn't just encouragement. It's equipment.
Because healing isn't a moment — it's a walk.

NOW AVAILABLE:

www.amazon.com

Welcome to the Faith Clinic: Stress Edition — where we don't hand you cute verses and clichés. We hand you spiritual prescriptions for real pressure, real panic, and real prayers from tired believers holding it together by a thread.

This book is for the overwhelmed—those trusting God while juggling bills, burnout, hustle culture, and holy frustration. If you've ever whispered, "God, are You even watching this mess?" this is for you.

Inside you'll find raw, soul-hitting chapters like:

- "God, I Trust You — But These Bills Keep Coming"
- "If Rest Is Holy, Why Does It Feel Like Slacking?"
- "I'm Tired of Smiling So You Won't Worry"

This isn't fluff. It's real talk for real stress—and a reminder that you're not forgotten, you're being fortified.

The Faith Clinic is open. Breathe in & take your spiritual vitamins. Healing begins here.

NOW AVAILABLE:
www.amazon.com

This isn't just a feeling — it's a flare signal from the soul. You pray, serve, and believe in God, but something deep inside is still simmering. Welcome to the Faith Clinic: Anger Edition — where suppressed emotions meet sacred intervention.

In this volume, Dr. Patricia S. Tanner guides you through spiritual triage for:

☑ Silent rage and emotional suppression

☑ The grief–anger connection

☑ Rejection wounds from childhood to church hurt

This isn't a lecture. It's a spiritual detox. No shame. No sugar-coating. Just raw, honest healing. Whether you're snapping at loved ones or silently seething under the surface, this book meets you at the boiling point—and leads you to the breakthrough.

🩺 This is the clinic.

💧 This is your moment.

And God is ready to heal the anger behind your amen.

NOW AVAILABLE:
www.amazon.com

In this powerful installment of the Faith Clinic series, Dr. Patricia S. Tanner brings biblical insight, emotional compassion, and spiritual strength to those walking through grief. Designed as a healing chamber for the soul, each "dose" of this devotional targets a different dimension of sorrow—guiding you from pain to peace, from mourning to joy.

Inside, you'll discover:

- Daily doses of Scripture-based encouragement.
- Personal reflections and prayers for each stage of grief.
- Practical faith prescriptions to help you process loss and find purpose.

Whether you are navigating the recent loss of a loved one, confronting buried grief from the past, or supporting someone else in their sorrow, this devotional offers a gentle yet powerful roadmap to healing. Come, take your seat in the Faith Clinic—where the Great Physician is ready to restore your soul.

NOW AVAILABLE:

www.amazon.com

30 Days Of Grieving

Given By The Inspiration Of God

Healing From COVID-19

Almost a year later, it hit me... My mother was gone, and I was still stuck at the hospital. I had tried everything from crying to counseling, and even prayer. Pray they told me. Trust God they insisted. But it seemed as if nothing was working. I was hurt, dealing with my reality: my mother was not coming back.

While journeying through grief, it was under the divine 'Inspiration of God' that He placed me in a trance. While I was gaining a revelation about grief, He gave me this journal, '30 Days Of Grieving.'

NOW AVAILABLE:

www.amazon.com

The 30 Days Challenge:

I Tested POSITIVE for COVID-19

If you had 30 days to live, what would you do? If you were told that you needed to prepare for a marathon in 30 days and you were completely out of shape, what would you do first? If a family member handed you one million dollars and told you that you had to figure out how to build a house (debt free), how would you execute your plan?

I'm catching you off guard with these requests, right? Well, this is exactly what COVID-19 did when it snatched my mother's life away, wrecking my entire world. I had to battle for my mother AND my faith in 30 days flat. What a challenge!

Throughout this book, I will walk you through my brief journey with COVID-19, negative of a happy ending. I will share the diary I kept while attending to my mother, and the scriptures I read, prayed, and quoted as my shield and protection.

Take the journey with me, there is healing on the other side!

NOW AVAILABLE:

www.amazon.com

Can Salvation Get You Into Heaven? The Answer Is Yes! offers a powerful and biblically grounded exploration of God's eternal plan, revealing the heart of the Gospel and the assurance of salvation through Jesus Christ.

 Unpacking life's most vital questions—Who is God? Why were we created? What does Jesus' life mean for us?—this book brings clarity to the believer's journey and confirms that salvation, once received, is eternally secure.

Whether you're seeking understanding or affirming your faith, this inspiring guide will lead you into the confidence and joy of knowing heaven is your eternal home.

NOW AVAILABLE:

www.amazon.com

The Bench That Waited is a bold and prophetic call to action for believers who've grown comfortable in church attendance but stagnant in purpose.

With raw honesty and spiritual insight, Patricia Tanner exposes the quiet crisis of passive faith—where callings are delayed and obedience is optional.

Through Scripture, stories, and reflection, this book urges readers to rise from routine, break free from spiritual stagnation, and step boldly into their Kingdom assignment. The bench has waited long enough—will you?

NOW AVAILABLE:

www.amazon.com

What happens when the Kingdom becomes a stranger?

The Godless Climb is not a rejection of faith—it is a raw, unflinching journey through what remains when belief unravels. With brutal honesty and tender grace, this book explores the spiritual free fall that follows the loss of divine certainty, the ache of unanswered prayers, and the void left when God no longer feels near.

Written for those who have quietly slipped out of the pews and into a wilderness of doubt, grief, and inner searching, this is not a triumph story—but a survival story. A confession. A sacred wrestle. Through personal reflection and prophetic insight, the author unpacks what it means to climb without a safety net, to live without the scaffolding of religious performance, and to build a new compass in the absence of old crutches.

You haven't arrived. But you're still climbing. And that is holy.

NOW AVAILABLE:
www.amazon.com

It Was The God In

Me

Success can be attributed to many things. Depending on the person who has obtained success would determine those to whom they attribute their success. Some give credit to their daily routine while others give credit to a mentor or some sort of system they followed. When I think about my success, the only person who I can give the credit to is God.

In this memoir, I share the successes and failures I have experienced throughout my life. From my individual experiences to my entrepreneurial journey, I share how God has walked with me every step of the way.

Come and see.. It Was The God In Me!!

NOW AVAILABLE:

www.amazon.com

The Triple 7 Formula is designed for business owners who are looking forward to hitting the million-dollar mark in their business. If you own a business and seem to be running in financial circles, this book will get you on track to simultaneously gaining sound business structure and millions in your bank account.

It was through many conversations with business owners lacking financial gain that prompted Patricia to share her blueprint for millionaire status. Through this book, she demonstrates how to gain financial ground by developing strong teams, implementing systems, and setting stackable goals. If you are ready to gain a laser sharp focus, and implement these clear steps, you will position yourself for financial greatness. Your business will be sound, and you will see financial growth beyond your wildest dreams!!

NOW AVAILABLE:
www.amazon.com

The Triple 7 Formula is specifically crafted for business owners aspiring to reach the million-dollar milestone. If you are a business owner feeling stuck in financial cycles, this book will set you on the path to building both a solid business structure and financial success.

This workbook is designed to complement the textbook of the same name. As you progress through its pages, you will be inspired to take decisive steps toward becoming a millionaire. From constructing your business framework to creating the millionaire's avatar, this process will expand your knowledge and mindset. Not only will you chart a course to financial success, but you will also identify your accountability circle and select a mentor to guide you toward greatness.

I cannot guarantee millionaire status unless you actively follow the steps to begin your journey. If you are searching for a get rich quick scheme, this workbook is not for you. I am looking for those ready to put in the effort—and since you are reading this, I believe that's you!

You have finally found it: Your roadmap to millions!

NOW AVAILABLE:
WWW.Amazon.com

Find Patricia on The Web:

www.PatriciaTanner.com

Follow Patricia on social media:

Facebook & Instagram: @PatriciaTannerInc